The Voice of Truth

Memoirs of a Nurse

Christina Hunter

ISBN 979-8-89345-513-7 (paperback)
ISBN 979-8-89428-261-9 (hardcover)
ISBN 979-8-89345-514-4 (digital)

Copyright © 2024 by Christina Hunter

All rights reserved. No part of this publication may be reproduced, distributed, or transmitted in any form or by any means, including photocopying, recording, or other electronic or mechanical methods without the prior written permission of the publisher. For permission requests, solicit the publisher via the address below.

Christian Faith Publishing
832 Park Avenue
Meadville, PA 16335
www.christianfaithpublishing.com

Printed in the United States of America

To my beautiful mom, Michelle Marie Vitullo, who saved my life more than once and in more than one way. You are cherished, and I carry you in my spirit until we meet again.

Contents

Introduction vii
Chapter 1: Relativity as I Know It 1
Chapter 2: Sleeping Beauty 4
Chapter 3: Like a Scene from Grey's Anatomy 10
Chapter 4: Crowned the Pannus Princess 19
Chapter 5: An Attack of Mind, Body, and Spirit 25
Chapter 6: Surviving COVID and Trusting God to Be
 the Judge 34
Chapter 7: Informed Consent 42
Chapter 8: America the Beautiful 48
Chapter 9: Pressure On, Pressure Off 55
Chapter 10: What Am I Doing Here? 61
Chapter 11: Prevention versus Pathogenesis 68
Chapter 12: Being Different 81
Chapter 13: The Day My Mom Saved My Life 90
Chapter 14: The Beginning of the Letters 96
Chapter 15: The Meeting 128
Chapter 16: Continued Fight for Change: Letter 2 134
Chapter 17: Finding Purpose in the Moment 162
Chapter 18: The Day I Was Interrogated on the Job 168
Chapter 19: The Drug Search and Nurses Questioned 182
Chapter 20: Another Letter and the Meeting with Corporate 185
Chapter 21: The Fight Is Bigger Than Just Where I Am 201
Chapter 22: Why Are We Tolerating the Corruption? 204
Chapter 23: Fighting for Myself 208
Chapter 24: Learning How to Survive the Storm 211
Chapter 25: My Dad and Why He Is My Hero 219
Chapter 26: Hurry, Hide the Cups! 226
Chapter 27: The Day I Would See My New Life 232

Introduction

Have you ever asked yourself the question, What am I doing here? Have you ever questioned your purpose in life and really struggled to find out who you really were? These questions burned within me every day as I walked into the hospital to start yet another long shift as a nurse. I began searching. Everyday living started to feel monotonous. My job as a nurse became unbearable. I lost interest in things that used to bring me pleasure. I wanted to find answers to so many questions about life, and that led me to the writing of this book. As I began not just living and going through the motions but instead writing down what happened through the days, the story of my life unfolded before my eyes, and I was able to finally learn truths and that I needed to find my place in this world. I traveled down so many roads that seemed desolate, and I wondered when I would finally reach a good destination. I became desperate to understand. Finally, I decided to be open-minded through times of hurt and chaos and overwhelming struggles like COVID, death of loved ones, debt, job instability, dead-end dreams, and moments of helplessness. I found that it was through these times that I was becoming who I was meant to be. Simple pleasures and understanding this world offers just weren't enough for me anymore. I needed more.

As a nurse in America, I struggled with knowing what was right in how patients and medical professionals were to be treated but seeing them treated poorly instead. I struggled as I saw how the sports world was changing, and suddenly, what I once knew about sports seemed far away. I began to disengage so that I could take a step back and evaluate what I was seeing in the workforce and even in our own families as a culture was developing that I wanted to pull away from. It seemed that so many were geared toward goals that were far from beneficial, and I realized that the world around me was a force that pulled toward a direction that was not sitting well within me and to a place I did not want to go. Why was this? Why was I not fulfilled in what the world around me offered? Why was I struggling to still find purpose even though I had a very busy life with a full schedule of events all the time? Why was I being faced with adversity as I exposed these truths to others in sports, nursing, and the school system? The more I learned, the further I honed in on a particular truth and was able to cut out distractions and get to the root of what it was I was searching for. I knew I was on to something. This is the story of my life as a nurse and how, through twenty years of service, I am still learning about life, love, and sacrifice.

When you can see yourself as the only one of you and know that you have a specific calling, you will be unsettled until you find it. I encourage you to search for that purpose in your own life that leads to peace, and I'll share with you the story of finding my own purpose, as it came to me one clue at a time, leading me into a true understanding of service, success, and profit. I share in this book how I was an advocate for patients, nurses, my kids, and even myself, and how this put a target on my back. This battle was relentless, and the world wages war on people who fight for truth. I will talk about how I learned to weather the storm, even in dark times, staying true to my roots and foundational faith that ended up bringing change after all. It did not happen the way I expected; it was better. I will tell of the power of the change that comes from within and how believing in what you know is true will set you free and will lead to abundant blessings, steering you down the right path to victory.

Chapter 1

Relativity as I Know It

During the times of the COVID "crisis," general rules of nature became clearly ignored by some and respected by others in our country. For every action that takes place in our lives, there are multiple people affected as a result of our decisions. This follows the rules of natural law and relativity, which were designed by God. I saw many people removed from the roots of their morals and once valued high-standard levels of thinking during times of distress and fear of the unknown. I also saw other people shift in a different way and desire a higher level of living, choosing to reroute their lives to live with purpose during times of distress. I will tell stories of inspiration that came from my patients, even those in a forever sleep, stories that changed me and can change you too. I choose to take my role as a nurse seriously and to give a voice to those who cannot speak for themselves but have so much to say.

Have you ever wondered why them? Why me? Have you ever thought that a good person had something bad happen to them and it did not seem fair, while others who do not seem deserving get rewarded in life? From the beginning of time with Adam and Eve in the garden of Eden, decisions were made by each of them that changed everything for the whole. God chose those two to be at the top. Now, in this frame of time in creation, God is still supreme, and people at the top of our system of leadership are still tasked with making decisions that affect the whole. This does not mean that we must see ourselves as victims, though. Throughout the Bible, God teaches of men and women who came along in this plan of nature and whose decisions had big effects. This is still true today. I will tell stories of how I fought COVID in ways that were not popular and won. I will talk about how I fought to keep people in their jobs while maintaining their autonomy, faith, and self-worth, and they pressed on. I will also tell of how authentic leadership is witnessed through inspiring others to become innovative and how transformational leadership is what has built and sustained our country and is what is needed to get the most out of jobs of service.

God is writing our stories each day. What is he writing about you? What has he planned for you? We are all accountable for making big changes to the world around us, whether good or bad. COVID is just one of the topics discussed in this book to help us see that we all will be part of cause and effect, and the lives we live are relative to an ultimate plan. We need to stay focused, all of us, individually as we influence the families we represent by blood but also who we meet and represent every day by the power resulting from our actions regarding them.

I will share my perspective from the bedside as a registered nurse in America. I learned so much from my patients, even ones who could no longer speak. Through their silence, I learned the power of my voice and theirs. I learned how to listen to people when they say nothing at all.

My family is directly affected by my decisions as a parent, wife, nurse, and every other role I take on, and it is my job and my honor to stay grounded in a belief system that represents faith, integrity, honesty, and loyalty. Maneuvering through our jobs every day when the focus of our leaders is the profit of money first has created a shift in our country's value system. Even if the idea is to "provide for your family," putting profit of money over people will never benefit our country; and as the law of nature proves, this kind of desire for control will only cause us to fail. If we look back to the story of Adam and Eve, we learn this has been a problem from the beginning, and people who are deceived continue trying to create a system that seems successful but one God will never approve of. As big corporations push to serve self and look for ways to gain more power and control, and others are trying to compete in the business, God remains supreme. The good news is that God turns all things into good for those who love him and are called according to his purpose. As we support the idea that we all are relative to each other and were made to work together, we can understand that just like Adam and Eve did when they were forced from the lush and beautiful garden of Eden, we too will be keeping blessings from coming by our negative acts. It may seem like we have the right to take things for ourselves and that as long as we are successful according to the world's system of value, and comfort, we are doing all right. COVID allowed our country to be sifted like miners do in search of gold. Miners search through dirt and debris to find those valuable pieces of gold. As our country gets sifted, people and truths of value are revealed and are cut away from the distraction of disease and oppression. This is what our country is going through, a sifting. I hope to influence others to desire to be found by God as valuable and, through our experiences, to be useful and to be part of something truly profitable, which is to understand profit on a higher level. I hope you enjoy these stories and that you find your purpose.

Chapter 2

Sleeping Beauty

Fight for understanding. Press into discomfort, even crave it, because this is what brings about the change in you.

My version of the story of "Sleeping Beauty" is different from the fairy tale you may have heard before. This is the story of a young woman I took care of at the hospital several years ago as a nurse on an intermediate medical-surgical step-down unit. This story helped me understand the power of love and prayer that supersedes physical place, actual time, and perceived circumstance. This experience was foundational in my life as I learned from the beginning of my career as a nurse how to transfer power and love from one to another.

During a very regular shift, I got word that I would be getting a transfer as my new admission. This patient was a trauma victim coming from the ICU. I was given some information in advance concerning her condition so I could set her room up appropriately and have everything ready for her arrival to the unit. I got busy preparing to have things in place that I would need to provide proper care. I went through the room as I normally would to prepare for my new admission, but I could not prepare myself for what I would encounter that day. I set up wall suction and got all needed supplies for trach care, catheter care, mouth care, oxygen, and the like—the whole nine yards. I often had patients who were medically intense when ICU was full and couldn't house the patients. I was comfortable caring for the high-level-of-care patients. I was told in report that this woman was weaned off the ventilator at this point and only required a high level of oxygen by mask to her trach tube, but she was unresponsive, severely impaired in terms of cognitive awareness, and in a vegetative state from injuries that she sustained in a recent car accident.

I set the room up, and then before she arrived, I received some of her personal items from the other unit. I began to unload the brown paper bag I was given that housed these items. As I looked down into the bag, my perspective completely changed. I was usually very professional and strategic at these times, mechanical and mentally tough, but what I saw when I looked in that bag caused me to pause as a softness came over my body. I could see lying right on top of everything in the bag a beautiful drawing made by a child. It was illustrated and carefully colored with every color in the rainbow. There were several smiling stick figures, and at the top of the portrait was written with a child's handwriting, "Get well soon, Mommy." I gently and with a sense of reverence, pulled the drawing out of the bag and taped the beautiful portrait on the wall, and then my curiosity heightened as I hesitated and then peered back into the bag. I carefully reached in and pulled out the next item. It was a framed polaroid picture of a woman with five children surrounding her. I held that framed picture in my hand and then began looking around the room at all the medical equipment that I set up. There was such a contrast between the medical equipment and the personal items of this young mom who would be coming down the hallway in her hospital bed any second. I began to tear up as I gently placed the framed picture on her nightstand. I began to pace the room knowing what I knew as a nurse and knowing what I would soon be seeing and dealing with. This was uncharacteristic of me. Normally, I separated myself from the patients emotionally so I could care for them without getting too attached. But this case was different. I remember having to turn off my emotions. I had a few kids of my own at the time and immediately identified with this young mom with young kids. I started praying right away. "Dear God, please help me to be able to take care of this woman." I started to panic a little. I had been a critical care nurse for a while, and I was comfortable taking care of trauma victims from a vast variety of situations. This should have been no different than any other day at work, but it was. For me, it was always about people. So all I could do was pray. *How could I help this one?* I thought.

They pushed her bed into the room, and that is when I met her for the first time. The transfer nurses and I got her set up. I looked at her knowing her injuries were life-altering. She had the signature incision across the entire right side of her head that was lined with staples, telling me the story of her craniotomy. Her condition told me things, and I was listening. The craniotomy was performed in hopes to relieve pressure after her brain had swelled from the closed head injury she sustained. After the trauma, the brain needed to rest and have room to expand to hopefully preserve its integrity. Her brain functioned enough to keep her alive but not to keep her conscious. The right side of her injured head was shaved. Out of the other side of her head flowed her very long beautiful hair that was caked to her head with old blood, telling me the story of her youth, vibrance, and beauty but also of that fateful day that changed her forever. My mind and medical experience told me she would never see her family again and would never be the same woman she was before the crash. She would never wake up from her forever sleep and would never again respond to the world around her. My heart was crushed, and I wondered how her little ones would be able to understand why when they called to her and said, "Mommy, wake up," she would not respond. When they asked, "Mommy, play with me," she would not get up and go to them. When they would say, "Mommy, hold me," but her arms did not reach for them, would they understand that she could not answer their request for her to continue loving them the way they were used to? I wondered why I was there with that woman that day, and although I felt helpless, I decided to love her in the ways I could. The way her kids would want me to love her.

Even if I never met her family, I knew they would want me to love their mom. So many times I found myself in rooms with patients who were in a coma, and I would ask God what I was doing there. He would tell me to love the patient, so I always got to work. I did not have control over who was a DNR and who was a full code. I did not have control over when a family decided or did not decide to turn off life support. I tried to love this mom but hated my boundaries, knowing I could not help her return to who she once was. I realize that absolute purity has no boundaries. It is free of restriction, so this was how I chose to love people like this. I always remain hopeful for patients even in the worst situations and even when there seems to be no hope because I leave them in God's hands.

In my years as an athlete, I learned through games that even when there seems to be no hope in winning, doing your best may surprise you with a win that was possible after all. In this situation, I made the decision to keep hoping that she and I had purpose in that moment. I dressed her wounds, kept her clean and breathing well, comfortable. I knew her kids would want me to take care of their mommy while she was in the hospital as they were figuring this new life out. So I loved their mom. With every breathing treatment, turn of her body, wipe of her face, and prayer over her, I would love her. This was how I could love them too. If they were at home praying that the nurses were taking good care of their mom, I wanted to help answer those prayers by taking good care of this woman. This was the hope I had in the situation and the only way I could see it. I chose to be positive and to remain optimistic, honest, and true to the situation. I chose to do what I could and not focus on the negative.

This experience was more than fifteen years ago, but I remember like it was yesterday. I never found out what happened to her. I never met her family. I took care of her a few times before she moved on, and I assumed she went to an extended care facility, but my hope was that she recovered and had a miraculous healing as this is always my hope for patients like this. I still think of her and pray for her and her kids and hope they all are having a blessed life. I wonder how old her kids are now, and over the years, I think of how they must be getting big. Nurses are not robots, but much is expected of them as they care for patients to learn to love them even from an uncomfortable position and even when things seem unfair. These patients stay in our hearts as we go through the day-to-day. Even writing this was hard for me. I always had the reputation of being tough, and not many things made me emotional. I act as I must and respond the best I can when called to action, but the fact remains that these patients touch our hearts and lives forever as we choose to love them from the bedside. I still remember this woman's first name to this day, which is crazy, since my kids tell me I have a "Rocky Balboa brain" because I never remember names of all their friends and they must remind me of dates and times of all their events. They do not understand how I forget so many things, but the truth is, my mind holds onto so much. This is how I see the imprint that was made on me through that encounter with my patient. She made such an impact on me, even in her beauty sleep. The story she told me and the lessons I learned through her would give me the momentum needed to be an advocate for truth.

I tell this story to tell of how experiences like this changed me. I used to be a yeller, getting loud at the simplest upsets to my comfort zone. I would clean the house to no end and needed things to be in their perfect places. Now things are different. I'm more flexible, and I don't worry as much about things that have no eternal value. If my little Christy, probably the age of one of this woman's kids at the time she had the accident, walks past me and gently swipes her hand across me, saying hello with her touch, but in the process knocks over my cup of coffee, making a mess of the carpet, I realize what I have that this woman does not have. I clean up the coffee with Christy beside me, thankful for the interaction between us even if it is just cleaning up a mess with my daughter. I used to yell and argue with my husband, but somehow being quiet makes more sense. Sometimes I do yell or get upset, but then I am reminded to check myself. It is these times that I think of that beautiful patient, "Sleeping Beauty," a mother I cared for all those years ago, who isn't able to clean up spilled coffee with her daughter but, instead, could not respond to her at all. She could not celebrate in her victories or comfort her in times of need. She cannot work out problems with her husband, making me believe that even in messes, I am blessed. That woman impacted me. She sharpened my conscience. Her story changed me, and that's what I want to do for others.

My life as a nurse allows God to knead me like dough. Just think of a pizza. You cannot add the toppings to the pizza dough until it is prepared or kneaded. Likewise, God must prepare us first to receive missions in life. As I had many experiences with patients and families over the years, searching for meaning and purpose in those times and reaching out to God for answers were necessary. I didn't know then what I know now. During these grueling experiences at the bedside, I realized, his hand was pressing into me as he was always teaching me and impressing on my mind and heart his purpose for me. He was working out all the imperfections of his dough, which was me. This process was uncomfortable because my nature is to judge people, to have an opinion, to see only one way, to push my own views on others, to be lazy, selfish, to have poor self-esteem and not think enough of myself, to be boastful, prideful, to hate others for any reason, to think too highly of myself...This is the nature of us all. God says we are born into this sinful world, so we must be taught and kneaded into the beautiful person God sees in us, his creation. He kneads out the ugly little by little and gives us self-confidence, a love for others, urgency to care, selflessness, gratitude, generosity, vision, a nonjudging heart, humility, unspeakable joy, thankfulness, wisdom, and understanding. This is what I hoped for after being in those rooms, taking care of people and their families, gaining these qualities and attributes of heart so I could bless others more. Even if we don't see the negative, it is within us, hiding. That is why God tells us to ask him to search us to find these negative things to weed out so we are not held back by evils we don't even realize are inside us. God's preparation of us is a process, and he is working out our kinks as we serve him. We all have a choice, and some nurses do not share the same thinking as I do. I know for sure that God can take us farther than we can take ourselves, and in this knowledge and understanding is power.

Chapter 3

Like a Scene from Grey's Anatomy

My foundation in critical care built me for my future in nursing, and for the most part, I loved what I did "for a living." It wasn't until the last couple years of service that I began really searching for more. I needed to have more passion to gear my efforts toward a direct target. This brings more power and meaning to our lives. My first orientation shift in the ICU during COVID pandemic was a life-changing event. I chose to go and work on this unit to help during a time of need and to shift in the opposite direction of fear and apprehension I saw surrounding the virus. I worked in obstetrics at the time on a mom and baby unit, but the atmosphere in the ICU brought back many memories of my nursing past. My preceptor and I had two patients that first day. These patients were positive for COVID and were in droplet isolation. They had their wrists restrained to the bed to prevent removal of their artificial airways, were in medically-induced comas with the use of IV propofol, and were mechanically ventilated. Both had feeding tubes. One was in normal sinus rhythm on the heart monitor with occasional bigeminy, and the other was in A-fib with slow ventricular rate. The doors to these rooms were glass, and we monitored them from the hallway to limit exposure to the virus. During COVID pandemic, one of the things that changed was the IV tubing. Nurses would add extension tubing to reach all the way from the patient in the bed to the hallway. The tubing would lay on the floor on top of disposable waterproof mats so they did not touch the floor, thereby honoring safety and health protocols. The glass doors would close, and the pumps then were operated, drip rates adjusted, and antibiotics, drugs, and fluids hung in the hallway to "limit exposure" of the nurses to COVID and to "preserve" the personal protective equipment. There were no nurse's aides on this unit, which I believe was a way for the hospital to cut costs. Nurses would have two or even three patients at times. We had two COVID patients my first day, which I thought was a heavy assignment. The nurses just seemed to go with the flow there and accepted the workload. There were agency nurses working on that unit because of the need for more staff. This hospital was underpaying me by several dollars an hour but were also canceling nurses for their scheduled shifts and, on top of that, pulling in contracted agency nurses, making double my pay or sometimes maybe even more. The margin of acceptability in treatment of an employee was growing by the minute it seemed, and there were no clearly defined standards or principles when it came to deciding a nurse's worth. There was an absence of common ground and a loss of communication throughout the system. There was a lack of organized structure in this facility that relatively affected everyone. We were busy all morning that first day, assessing sedation, turning, cleaning up the patients, and crushing meds to put down the patient's feeding tubes. Since there were no aides to help turn the patients, we used the lift equipment.

One patient had reportedly recovered from COVID, was sent home, and then was readmitted to the hospital recently with what was thought to be a relapse of the infection, and now he was worse off than before. He had been there for a while and not improving. It was time to try to ween him off the ventilator, but he did not tolerate this, so we began making plans for him to have a permanent airway put in his trachea, and the temporary oral airway discontinued. He was becoming a long-term patient, and this was very disappointing to me. This was the type of patient I would sometimes receive on the critical care unit before shipping them to an extended care facility. This man had been sick for so long, and I wondered why the treatment regime was not judged more harshly as it was not effective in making him better. There were plans to move his oral feeding tube to his abdomen to be made more permanent as well. It often appeared that we would just check things off the list in medicine. There was an algorithm for everything, and this trumped reasoning at times. Sometimes it seemed the medical field was set up for people to just act. Even when other options were available, they were not even considered; they just moved the person down the line like they were an object in a factory.

Before we knew it, the time was 11:00 a.m. That was when a rapid response team was called overhead from the COVID unit on one of the general floors. This means a patient was crashing and was being sent to us, in the ICU, to hopefully be stabilized. My preceptor took me to the room, and everyone started to quickly migrate to that area. The glass doors were opened wide as the patient was being rushed down the hall, his bed pushed swiftly by nurses, as orders were yelled out by the doctor and the organized chaos began. This was all too familiar to me, and I knew what was ahead. We garbed up; everyone quickly rushed to the COVID cart donning COVID gear, N95 face masks, yellow gowns, hair nets, and shoe covers. We got double-gloved, double-masked, shielded our faces, and greeted the man in the bed as they wheeled him into the place that would become a war zone as we battled for his life. At that point he was conscious. He was sitting up in the bed, looking at us and saying, "I am dying…I am dying." This burned through me like a knife on fire. His skin was dusky, his voice weak, and his eyes told me he was right. The man's body began telling me his story, and I was listening. His family should have been called. His wife should have been there by his side to catch a glimpse of him and to say those last words to him while he was awake. At that time they were keeping family away unless the patient was on death's door, a concept and policy I hated, and I was against it from the beginning because it was evil. Many times, family did not make it in time to say goodbye. The nurses said, "No, you are not dying today. We are here to help you." I know this was their intentions and their hope, and so once this claim was made, I swallowed hard and got right to it, eager to help save his life. The doctor spat out, "Put him in Trendelenburg! I need pressurized fluid now! He needs blood!" Everyone responded to the urgency, moving faster and faster as the natural adrenaline was pumping through our veins, and more people flooded the room to help. I was just a girl on orientation and wanted to stay that way, but I knew that was not who I had to be in that room on that day. I had instincts and a unique skill set that developed over the last eighteen years that I worked as a nurse, and a solid nursing foundation from my time spent in critical care. I knew how to operate in these scenarios; I just had to respond. I could not get caught up in the moment but, instead, do what I was trained to do. Coach Carl had just talked about cuttlefish in jump stretch class that week at the Y. Jump stretch was my workout class that I did alongside my kids. Coach Carl is someone who inspires in his classes, and I needed that in my life. A cuttlefish is a type of fish, which stays in solitary, and is thought to be like a chameleon, staying camouflaged under the sea. These fish are thought to be very intelligent creatures and thought to change their eating habits and their activities, such as migrating, based on their environment because they desire comfort. Therefore, it seems that they are decisively reactive to their surroundings based on sensual desires instead of remaining consistently responsive to outside stimuli. They like temperate waters. They do not like extremes. As we know in life, pressure and heat are used to form crystals and precious stones with layers of beauty like we see in the Moroccan geode. The geode stays buried under the earth for many years, being emptied of itself and made hollow from the gas, pressure, and heat. Then over time water and minerals pass through the microscopic holes in the rock, leaving behind sediment that turns to beautiful crystal over time. Pressure and heat are also used to design objects to be used as tools, such as knives or swords. Pressure and heat are a type of refinery used to create shape, texture, and solidarity. Coach Carl taught us not to be like the fish that are never really changing, growing, or adapting to anything new and are not willing to withstand pressure or harsh conditions but, instead, are comfortable remaining the same throughout their life cycles, which are relatively short. He said you should get warm when it is time to get warm and then cool off when it is time to cool off, knowing this is necessary to build beauty within. Temperature changes are important, and adapting to the different temperatures of life creates in us a weathered attitude that has a larger margin of receptibility. This allows us to be open-minded and willing to participate in society to be a better team player. It will make us better nurses, mothers, fathers, siblings, friends, and so forth. As we are willing to be put under pressure for positive personal growth, we can then foster an environment to facilitate this in others.

This is where my mind took me in that room. I knew my oldest daughter, Sabria, who was a legendary basketball player and a senior at West Point Military Academy, would tell me to act. She would tell me to do what I knew how to do. Suddenly, I heard her voice inside me say, "Go, Mom, find something to do!" I heard everyone in the room yelling, "Grab the crash car! Get the board behind him! What is his pulse? Get the leads on! Do we have a blood pressure?"

I grabbed a saline bag and just started squeezing, forcing the fluid into the man's vein. Then I started setting up pressurized bags. I put the liter of fluid bags into the sleeves hanging on the IV pumps and started pumping up the bulb that hung from it, creating constant pressure to the liter of fluid. I just started going from one thing to the next, owning the battleground I populated. The room was filled with highly experienced nurses and doctors, and the hall was filled too outside the door with everyone available on the unit, including the hospital supervisor. Everyone was there with one goal, to save this man's life, but other lessons would be learned that day. God is the author of life and death, and he already had a plan. We were there to do what we were called to do, and all of us had purpose. I was at the left side of the patient at his head and shoulder level. His vitals were dropping. His color was changing. He was losing consciousness.

"He is going out! We need to intubate! Start compressions!"

I thought, *Here we go!*

The heat was on. The code cart was cracked open and meds pulled. The respiratory team was establishing an airway and bagging him. His color was bad, and the doctor saw me from a distance, and saw that I was new. Our eyes locked, and I was immediately annoyed at myself because I know what they do to orientees! You should never make eye contact or stand out. I was supposed to blend in!

"You are new here, right?" he said from across the room.

I said, "Yes."

I knew the tests were coming. He asked me to get some kind of medicine, and I did not understand him. The other nurses knew his game, so they quickly responded since what he was asking for was not in the room and I would have to search for it and did not know my way around the unit. Another nurse took that order and let me continue to hold my ground. The doctor had ordered two units of blood, and the runners in the hall had arrived back at the room with it after getting it from the blood bank. I was not there to impress the doctor, and being forty years old at this point, probably older than him and an experienced nurse, I was not impressed with his tactics to wear me in, and I ignored his disrespect. I was a professional and there to do what I could and to follow orders so that is what I did. I grabbed the bags of blood and set them up in the rapid infusion pumps. I was not familiar with these pumps, but I responded as a team player and figured it out. A nurse yelled that another IV access line was established. One by one they were gaining more IV access. We had several peripheral sites in his arms, a central triple lumen line in his femoral artery, and finally had a triple lumen in the jugular. Then I heard the doctor yell for the albumin, and I saw the glass bottle sitting on the table, arriving at some point in the chaos. I grabbed it and spiked the bottle. I began programming the other IV pump. I was working fast, trying to remain calm and found the medicine in the pump and thought, *Twenty-five percent albumin, there it is.* I got that going and handed the tubing to the nurse so she could twist the tube into the hep-lock. The doctor said, "Set it to 999." So I adjusted the pump. He wanted to bolus this and just get as much fluid into the man as possible. Everything was fast and hard—pumping the heart and flooding the circulatory system. Before long, we had plenty of IV access with central lines that were established, and we had three different vasopressors hung and infusing. Nurses were pushing the crash cart meds, taking a report of the process, and running around the room. This was like a scene from *Grey's Anatomy*, and I thought, *How am I back at this place? I am an OB nurse!* Nurses were throwing tubing, wrappers, and empty fluid bags were tossed to the floor. It was like a tornado was going through the place, all with one goal, to save this guy's life. The doctor yelled, "Who has the sodium bicarb?"

One of the nurses responded, "I do right here, going in now!"

The doctor yelled, "What round is this? Is it time for epi?"

Another nurse yelled, "No, Doc, we got twenty more seconds!"

We had norepinephrine, dobutamine, fentanyl, vasopressin, epinephrine, sodium bicarbonate, blood, fluids, a volume expander, everything. After two hours, we finally got him stabilized enough. His heart was beating on its own, and he had a sustainable blood pressure. His color was better, and everyone cheered. It was enough for us to stop and get a chest X-ray to check placement of the airway. We knew he was bleeding and needed to get to the bottom of what was wrong. Everyone left the room except for a few of us getting the X-ray and cleaning up the room. The wife was on her way, and we knew if we lost him again, getting him back would not be easy, if even possible. After everyone left the room, and the man was stable, we could finally breathe. This was when I took a glance at his name band. Now there was a connection I made and prayed for him specifically. I watched, and as soon as we turned him, his heart rate began dropping; his blood pressure was dropping, down, down, down, so fast in a flash he was down to 30/20 and asystole flashing across the monitor. We flew open the glass doors again and yelled, "Code blue!" I grabbed the board from under the bed and placed it under his back, my preceptor began compressions. In flooded all the staff. The doctor yelled, "I need dobutamine now! We need more blood!" It was like déjà vu. I grabbed more blood and hung it. I looked out in the hallway, and everyone was just staring, and their faces were telling of what we were finally forced to accept. I saw the chaplain was now in the crowd, and the whole unit seemed to be losing hope in a good ending. God's plan is always good even when we do not see it that way. I was praying for the man, and now was such a precious time in his life. The most precious.

"We have gone through two code carts, Doc," said a nurse.

The doctor looked around the room and said, "Well...that is it. That is all we can do." He paused and said, "We have nothing else to try. We have used everything we can. We must call it. Shut everything off."

He called the time of death, and I had looked down at the patient, and that name is forever etched in my mind. Everyone just stopped. There was a silence, a pause. This was the cooling that comes after the heat. We had the heat and pressure of trying for three hours to save this guy, and now the room was calm, quiet, still, and cold. I prayed for him as he crossed that bridge to Jesus and realized the man was right; after all, he was dying. He knew. All we were doing was working on this man's body while he was walking toward eternity. My hope was that all that time we spent in that room, working on this man's physical body and praying, God was working on his soul. For some reason, he needed that time. I believe we gave him that time with God to figure things out. Sometimes people need that. This is my hope, that our efforts meant something. A nurse started picking up trash and throwing it down, obviously disgusted with what just happened. Sometimes nurses blame themselves or just get upset over what seems to be a loss. I had a different outlook. It was his time. God took him. Did we do all we could for him? This question should always be asked. Could we have done anything better, different? We have control over how we do things, and we need to be accountable for our actions in life because how we live and our actions do matter. A life being taken when it is time is the work of God, and we do not have control over that. We finished cleaning up the room, and then my preceptor looked up at me and motioned me out of the room, leaving the man's admission nurse to finish getting his body ready for his wife. We went back to our other patients and continued where we left off with our other two COVID patients.

Later, after that shift, I went to jump stretch, and that class was therapeutic. How nice it was to breathe outside of that N95. Coach Carl didn't know how much of an impact his classes made on me and how important this time was for me to clear my mind. I called my dad later and let him know that was one of the worst days of my life. I chose to enjoy the simple things like my daughter Theresa, fighting for the front seat, and my oldest, Sabria, telling me about her basketball practice at West Point and how her shot was "water" and how she was so happy about that. Her basketball team was in isolation at the time, in a hotel at West Point. They had gone in and out of isolation whenever they would get exposed to COVID, and this was an intense time for them. Sabria vented to me so many times about how the isolating was so tough. When they were together as a team, basketball once again was a release for them. Something to have that was familiar, consistent, a tangible hope. This is what basketball should be. This was what jump stretch was for me. It was a release. Sports should not be a reason for gloating and taking a stand for self-worship, which is the turn basketball has unfortunately taken, but some are still trying to preserve the dignity of the game.

    I did not support the shutdowns or the isolating and still was not afraid of the virus. I got home that night and sat in the bath and just cried. I did not know if I could continue with this job. So many things about it were unsettling. I had texted my boss from mom and baby unit and told her I was not sure I would go back to the ICU. I really did not see much better things going on in my unit either. I didn't fit in, and I couldn't file these thoughts anywhere. I couldn't make sense of it. Later I would find out the truth that I was growing out of my position as God was building me for more. At that time I just kept doing my best, not knowing what was coming but believing someday things would make more sense. I told my boss that I had a rough day, and she said, "Were you in that code?" I told her yes, and she told me she was so sorry. She and my coworkers heard the code called overhead. They found out I was in that room, and they all said they were sorry. Nurses know nurses. Sometimes it is nice to go out after a rough shift and just talk about the day we had, and other times it is better to talk about something else, but having people who know what you know and have been where you have been is somehow comforting. It is like coming home. That is what jump stretch was for me, and that's what I hoped to be for others, a homecoming.

Chapter 4

Crowned the Pannus Princess

That night in the bath, as I just cried out to God for some relief, I thought about how I was not in a good situation at home. My husband, Bobby, was distant, and I was struggling to stay in the marriage. Now I understand things differently. I know that love is to be given, always, even if it is not reciprocated, but at that time, I craved more from him. That night Sabria texted me and told me she shopped from Aldi online and got groceries sent to her hotel. She was going to make spaghetti squash that night. Even with bags under her eyes and her spirits tested, she was still working hard to do what she could to remain positive there at the military academy. She was taking initiative to do what she could for herself while in isolation. She also told me she bought Christmas presents for her five siblings online with some of her savings, and the packages were being sent to my house. This was encouraging to me, and this helped me see that others have hard times too but they press on, and this could be done by loving others. I had one shift on the mom and baby unit, and then the next time I went into work, I walked down the hall and heard, "I am sorry, Tina, but you are going down to the ICU." I said, "Oh, that is fine, no problem." It was either go to ICU or get canceled to stay home without pay. I smiled and went on my way, thankful to have a job to take care of my family while taking care of other people's family. I did not want to see this as a job or way to make money. I had to know there was more to it, and I believed God was building me for more. I wanted my coworkers to know that they could do things too that seemed scary or out of their comfort zone and they could do it without being sad or complaining. This was who I had to be.

During report, outside of our COVID patient's room in ICU, my preceptor looked and said, "Oh, I do not like that blood pressure." Our patient's blood pressure was dropping, and her heart rate was increasing. She was normally in A-fib with slow ventricular rate, but now the rate was much higher. She was not tolerating whatever was going on in her body. Even in a coma, she began telling us a story, and I was listening. Her white blood cell count had jumped up, and her breathing was worse. She had fluid in her lungs, which prevented proper flow of oxygen and created more pressure buildup, pushing her into an acidotic state according to her blood gases. If we did not act quickly, she would go into cardiac arrest. Her labs, vitals, and blood gases were all bad. Suddenly, more nurses came and were waiting with us outside the room, and I looked around and thought, *Oh no, not this again. Here we go.* My idea of ICU so far was patients crashing and COVID everywhere. My preceptor said, "We have to get in there." I put my COVID garb on and looked at the manager and the doctor who were standing there too, outside of the room. This doctor was the same guy from the other day in the code blue room. When I looked at him, I had visions of compressions and hanging blood and clapping and cheering and then devastation. He was the one who tested me after asking if I was new there. I looked at him and tried to lighten the mood a bit since he had already been there for twenty-four hours straight at that point. I knew they looked at me and remembered me from the other day, so I smiled and said, "I think I bring a black cloud with me." They both laughed and said, "Yeah, I think it is your fault. You were here the other day when that guy crashed." They both seemed to relax a bit after that. I knew we were a team, and none of us wanted to be there at that moment under those circumstances and in that situation, but there we were. We needed to use all our resources, get comfortable with each other, and try and help this person. I got all my garb on and went in. We no longer had central line access because that site was taken out through the night and the tip cultured as infection was suspected. So we were at a loss already without enough IV access to do what may need to be done. The night shift nurse did not expect the patient to start to crash, but the patient started going downhill fast. She was teetering on the line of going into congestive heart failure and was in kidney failure, so we had to be careful to not overload her with fluid. The manager brought the crash cart into the room, and we decided to cardiovert the patient to hopefully shock her into a better rhythm. We attached the pads and turned on the machine to sync mode. The manager yelled for everyone to "clear!" Then the patient was shocked with two hundred joules. The patient's whole body jolted, and her heart converted to normal sinus rhythm. Again, we clapped in the room and cheered. "All right!" The doctor would attempt to access an arterial line into her femoral artery to watch her mean arterial pressure to give us a more accurate reading of her blood pressure. He had the drapes over the patient, and I was there to assist. I was called "the pannus princess" that day because my job while the doctor was trying to insert the line was to hold up the patient's skinfold that lay over the top of her femoral artery. He had to use ultrasound to visualize the artery and still maintain sterile field. I was sweating and getting a good workout that day. He tried to lighten the mood by asking me if I did Pilates and then told me this exercise of holding up the pannus was considered "nursing Pilates." I had to laugh a little as I rolled my eyes at him as sweat was dripping down my back and my muscles were trembling. I was leaning up against the bed holding this patient's skinfolds up, which seemed like forever as I huffed and puffed through that N95, gown, in double gloves, hairnet, and plastic face shield. I felt the burn and sweat beading all the way down my posterior chain. This procedure was quick, though. We hustled, trying to get her into a better state before we found ourselves in a worse scenario. Then another doctor came in and worked on the opposite side to put in a central catheter, and she was laughing at how sweaty she was. She was sweating through her pants. She was so hot. She had two gowns on. One for COVID and one for the sterile procedure. They worked so hard in there, getting a central line access and inserting an arterial line. People did not know how hard of a job that was under the circumstances and pressure, but nurses and doctors pushed themselves to just do the job well and accept the negatives surrounding it, like almost passing out from the heat. I was impressed with the doctors and nurses there. Finally, the central lines were in. We had the patient on norepinephrine or (Levophed) and phenylephrine to control her blood pressure, and then we started antibiotics. We did give her some fluid, but she was on dialysis and in renal failure, so this was working against us, and we needed to adjust things accordingly to protect her kidneys. Considering her high white blood cell count and rapid change in vitals, sepsis was the concern. We were able to shut off her heparin drip since she was no longer in A-fib, and we continued with propofol for sedation while on the ventilator and fentanyl for pain control and comfort. She was still acidotic, so respiratory came to adjust her ventilator settings to hopefully get her out of this phase and get her lungs and body to better profuse with oxygen. It was a never-ending battle with her, but for the time being, she was stable.

The other patient we had was next door, and he was the same man from the other day who had a relapse of COVID who was getting transferred to a step-down unit. He had permanent placement of his feeding tube, and his oral airway was transferred to the trachea. We were now weaning him off the propofol so he could be transferred to a step-down unit. This was another tough day, but God was there. He was there when I suctioned that patient's lungs. He was there in the other room as I reached under the bed to untie that patient's wrist restraints so that I could pull her up in bed. He was there when I crushed those meds and was careful to put them into her feeding tube, not clogging the line. He was there as I was trembling to hold up her skin so the doctor could get good visualization to place her lines. He was there as I looked at her monitor and learned to titrate her drips to keep her in the safe zone. He was there when we shocked her into a better rhythm and the doctor said, "See what a little electricity could do?" God was always there, never letting nurses go at it alone, and that is what kept us coming back. The next few weeks in the ICU were intriguing. I continued to learn how to chemically paralyze a patient and why it was important at times. I learned that proning a patient with COVID helps to expand the alveoli in the posterior lungs, which facilitates better oxygen saturation for the blood, tissues, organs, and muscles. The proning of a patient involved about five nurses who would go into a room and turn the patient onto their abdomens. This was a tough technique, and nurses had to be very careful in doing this to maintain all their lines and tubes and to keep them safe from spontaneous extubation. It was hard on the patient too. Sometimes drip rates, sedation, and vent settings would need to be adjusted to support this type of treatment. The patient would remain in this unnatural position, face down, for eighteen hours straight. The ventilator did all the breathing for the patient. A tube went from the nose to the stomach to rest the upper gastrointestinal tract. Tubes were in place to rest the lower bowel, bladder, and lungs so that all these systems were rested during this time. The tubes measured the core temperature of the patient. It was a very complicated arrangement, and the negative ended up being the necrosis that appeared on the body at pressure points from this unnatural position. No matter how many pillows were pushed under the face, or pressure dressings were placed, or position changes were made, the skin, which was just not built to handle this, would turn black at the points where no circulation was getting into the skin. Patients would get that signature black nose that resulted from the lack of circulation to that area. It was just an acceptable setback for what was hoped to be gained from the treatment. I saw this as torture, and I just had to believe there was more that could be done to help COVID patients. It seemed like we were behind the times and just chasing the effects of COVID instead of being ahead of it and ready to take it on. We were just inching these people to the end. It seemed like a slow death. Why weren't we killing the virus first and then working on the repair of the damage? I had seen people recover from COVID when it was treated appropriately, and then I saw people suffer and die when other problems existed or when it seemed that the target was off. Some cases, I do believe, could have been better managed, but by the time people reached the hospital, they were facing more than just COVID. COVID could be hard on all the systems, and depending on the person's weakness and overall health, it could be devastating. I began to hear that hospitals were only permitted to use certain meds and treatment regimens that were "approved." This word really has been used to promote evil. People with no conscience are approving things for our country, and this needs to be looked at. This was a time when a certain "vaccine" could be used that was not approved at first, but treatments that were proven to heal COVID victims were not allowed in the hospital. Families were kept out, which should have never been tolerated. People did not have full awareness of what their loved ones went through and what was being done for them. The evil involved in all of this was evident from the very beginning. I was an advocate for autonomy, and I helped people to apply for religious exemption and keep their jobs in the hospital without getting the COVID vaccine. I spoke on the radio station and was on the news to try to take a stand for what I knew was right in promoting freedom and good health.

Chapter 5

An Attack of Mind, Body, and Spirit

I decided not to continue working in the ICU. I did not agree with all that was going on there and what nurses were made to be a part of, but I appreciated all I learned and was able to grow through. Certain experiences in my life, like a surgery that I had that took me longer to recover from than expected, pushed me to focus more on my family, my health, and my marriage. If I did not have these, I did not have anything. This was a time to recalibrate my life compass and to self-reflect, and I took advantage of it. God needed to be my continued source of light, and he was working on me to understand and grow.

    Thankfully, my husband finally started to see me. He encouraged me and supported me through the elective surgery that I decided to have. Even though it was during COVID pandemic and many elected surgeries were not going off, I was able to have mine, and my doctor never judged me for not getting the vaccine and did not let it interfere with my surgery. He took great care of me and called me one of his all-time favorite patients. My husband was there by my side. He was not allowed to stay overnight and was hesitant to leave but followed instructions. He was very different now than he was in the past. He invested in taking good care of me. The next morning, he came into my room while a flood of nurses rushed in, and he did not know what was happening. While attempting to get out of bed for the first time after surgery, my blood pressure dropped to 70/40, and I almost went unresponsive. They started fluids and laid me back down. I usually have a hard time recovering from anesthesia, and I scared my doctor and my husband but ended up being fine. After this and some significant crossroads that we encountered in our marriage, Bobby was a different man. Suddenly, he did not leave my side. He washed my hair, brought me food, helped me to the bathroom, and nursed me back to health. It took a little longer than expected for me to recover, and I believe this was so Bobby and I could bond and I could clear my mind. It was God's planning. My surgery was extensive, and so was the repair we needed in our family. Bobby and I started working out together in the gym, and he lost over a hundred pounds. We decided to see even during COVID pandemic that our circle and support system is so important, and we decided to embrace that circle and invest more in it by seeking God's direction for our lives. This was how we could then serve others better.

People are making decisions that impact our lives. We all make impacts whether deliberately or unintentionally, and the result can be good or bad. Some believe working to obtain a degree gives them better schedules and bigger paychecks, which is a plus and will always result in good for their families. What you decide as profitable will shape your family and will put you on a course in life. As I maneuvered, as a nurse, through this difficult time in American history, I learned a lot about people and was reminded of a saying I was taught from a young age, "You don't work, you don't eat." Rely on God's strength, have regard for the weak, and take care of those in need. This only scrapes the surface of the appropriate response to human civilization, but it gives a basic understanding of doing your part and seeing others before yourselves. This system of moral principle has gotten pushed to the wayside in business and in sports. I heard it said by a local politician and military veteran that you should be focused more on pushing the wagon or pulling it, but not very often should you be riding in it. People are now taught from the top down to take for themselves and to live the easiest life ever, feeding selfish desires, which is termed as success, and this is now recognized in our country as leadership, reflecting a person having good mental health and self-worth. This is false teaching and a dangerous viewpoint. The godly principles of doing your part and recognizing the difference between the vines and the branches and knowing you fit somewhere on the tree have been tossed out. Now the thinking is the more popular you are, the better, so strive and compete to be liked, and not for anything important but for things like maintaining a certain body type or making lots of money. What happened when everyone panic-shopped because they were afraid of the virus? They went out and spent all their money on food and stocked up on items they did not need at the time but were worried they would need them at some point in the future. Or they worked out at the gym all day instead of going to work, making their bodies their god, and building popularity on social media and being highlighted as role models for our youth. It was every man for himself, but the media called it being united. I understand that some people were trying to protect their families in this, but God always provides for us, and there is a difference between us taking this on ourselves or trusting him and his plan for us. The government shut down jobs, so people did not have money to pay their rent; but they had a house full of food, toiletries, and all kinds of things, keeping people comfortable at home watching life from the TV and Internet. Eventually, people relied on the government to pay for rent too, and when they got that money, they foolishly squandered it on things that were not essential and then still did not have rent money. Then they asked the government for extensions on their house payments, car loans, and college tuition; and these wishes were granted. Is it true that paper money has no gold to support it in this country? We are so far in debt, and yet financial rescue was in full swing. I did not believe it. What would be asked of us in return when all things went back to normal? Would there ever be a normal again? We have not been living right from the beginning, but now we see the effects. People wanted to blame the fact that they did not have money on the coronavirus. The cycle of blame and worry went full circle and just continued. Banks got involved and gave out loans to people who got money from the government, but when this money ran out and people could not pay their loans, the banks had to get rescued by the government too. How long would this last? People depended on the government for information, medicine, food, housing, and jobs. Now people struggled to even think for themselves and stopped problem-solving all together. The struggle came from them giving in to their own fear and giving in to the desire to do whatever they wanted, whenever they wanted and believing comfort was key. They lost vision of what true leadership was, so if people called themselves humble or trustworthy, people believed them, even though their actions told another story. People began believing in this genie in a bottle that would grant them their wish for money when they ran low. They had no real right to do so but rather believed in the fantasy that they were being responsible for their health by not going to work, storing up for disaster, staying away from people, taking money they did not earn, overindulging at the expense of others, or gaining that perfect body to flaunt while others were fighting for the country's freedom. Discipline was going out the window, and we would have trouble getting out of that rut later. In fact, not only would we not get out of the rut, but people would get glorified for taking for themselves in a time of crisis, and our country called it a good investment and labeled them as good leaders. I am not without blame. God teaches we are all in need of grace. I made my own mistakes during this time, and I prayed for direction and forgiveness as I maneuvered through. This was a learning experience that I'm thankful for because I did try to reason out what was going on.

 My husband, Bobby, still worked through this time, but his boss cut down his hours so his company could save money even though the owner had gotten specific money from the government to make sure his workers got taken care of during this time and did not have financial burden. Bobby did end up having financial burden since he never saw that relief money, while his hours were still cut, and his boss supposedly pocketed the money or used it to further invest in his own company. This corruption was going on all over the world and seemed to start with the top leaders and administrators of America and trickling all the way down, but we all play a part in our country's struggle. We just want to blame our leaders. People were taking off work and getting paid more money to stay home than they were making to go to work, which only made America's work ethic even weaker. This was not only seen in the workforce but in schools and in sports too. People always looked for reasons to work less and vacation more. My husband lost hours and was prevented from working overtime so his boss could keep the relief money he got from the government. He wanted to keep the workers' overtime money and keep workers at work, giving them enough hours so he did not have to pay unemployment. Greed was growing at a fast rate. Nurses were still going to work and not getting the opportunity to stay home with pay, initially. This was the case where I worked. I never wanted to stay home anyway and did not see it as productive or opportunistic. I was made out to be a "hero" or "essential worker" when I considered it what it really was, my duty and everyone's duty, to work and provide a service. I decided to remain in the reality that I was made to serve others. If I did not work, I should not eat. Second Thessalonians 3:10 teaches on this. God is our provider, but doing our part teaches responsibility and discipline. Some people needed money, but some people needed affection, company, and the fellowship of others, which was also being suppressed. Lacking this type of socializing can negatively impact one's health even to the point of suicide, which was reportedly on the rise during this time in our country.

One of my dad's brothers was living in a group home where he could be looked after since he could not completely care for himself. My dad told my grandma, on her deathbed, a few years before the pandemic, that he would take good care of her son after she was gone. My grandma had six sons, but she was most concerned about this one. She was particularly worried about him since she was the last living parent and knew she would soon be dying, leaving her son without any parent or the ability to take care of himself. This one brother of my dad's that she worried about was in his sixties and suffered from mental retardation. He has the mind of a small child. He is a sweet soul, and his biggest passions are celebrating his birthday, eating cake, barbeque chips, and drinking sweat tea. He lives his best life when he gets to go out to lunch with my dad at one of his favorite food places and usually, he chooses KFC. Although a grown man on the outside, he remains a child inside. My dad is his best friend and support person. He lived in a facility for most of his life where he could be watched 24-7 and cared for if a need came up. He did have some chronic health problems but took medication and was able to live his life and remain active. During the pandemic, new restrictions went into order, and he was not allowed to visit with family or leave the facility as was his regular routine since he was a young boy. He did not have the mental capacity to understand what social distancing meant. He struggled with this concept since his mental understanding is that of about a five-year-old. He felt abandoned by my dad at times, even though my dad called the facility and begged to see my uncle, even setting up conference calls and meetings to ask to be allowed to even just have lunch with his brother or to take him out for a while, which the facility still prohibited. All visiting was halted, and the place was on lockdown, which was a poor decision by our leaders, and there is no excuse. My dad even tried to visit him through a window at the facility, but this was also hard to understand and broke my uncle's heart. He soon refused to eat and drink and even take his meds. His best moments were spent with my dad getting away from the group home and being with his family, but this was taken from him because of fear and lack of respect that was blamed on a virus. My uncle ended up depressed and was admitted to the hospital several times through the time of the pandemic, not for COVID but for relapses of his health problems, which I do believe were directly related to social distancing. Mind, body, and spirit are all connected to make up the whole person. This is a crime that people are treated this way out of fear and self-righteousness, and our country was allowing this to continue on. They were labeling the COVID illness as worse than mental illness, which was not true, and both can lead to death. This is what caused me as a nurse to question their motives. I was baffled, but I understand greed and power, and the love and obsession of both were used to steer our country in the wrong direction. It is selfish for people to spread the disease of social distancing, which is just as powerful as the sickness that comes from a virus. Both are toxic. Both are spreading evil, and both lead to death. I am familiar with the widespread epidemic of abuse that goes on in facilities who house people who do not have the mental capacity to protect themselves. Sick-minded people do prey on the "weak" to satisfy selfish, evil desires and agendas, and this sickness is as toxic as COVID. This was a true concern for my dad as he wanted to protect my uncle. This country chose to lift the COVID situation as a point of focus, even worshipping it as a god and letting it run lives. People even used it to make tons of money, making a mockery out of those who suffered during this time. If you keep yourselves oppressed by only seeing the challenge directly in your face as having more power than your foundational faith and principles, then you are not choosing to be a leader but blindly following those who are on missions even if those people are on a mission to self-destruct. My dad struggled with not being able to be near his brother as he remembered promising their mom on her deathbed that he would always look after him. There is no excuse for the suffering that came to my dad and his brother, and not even fear of COVID excuses the abuse that took place because of senseless regulations and heartless people. The medical field was teaching how to live in dishonor and promoting this kind of life by keeping families separate and giving medical misinformation.

Administrators and people allowed things to go on because they didn't want to stand out or be looked at as a pot stirrer. They wanted to keep their cushy jobs and their nice paychecks, so they allowed things to continue. Still, I know that God will work all things out for the good because those who love him have this promise, and this is what I clung to as my family was abused during this "crisis" as many of us were. We must remember that we do have a choice to get involved where and when God gives us opportunity. God gives life and takes it; that is his right, but what goes on in between, he gives us power in. It is how we respond to things that makes the difference. Many people were getting medical attention over the phone and even being misdiagnosed or not diagnosed at all. I heard of kids who were showing up to the E.R. with high fevers and sent home without proper treatment. One story I heard of was of a child who had been positive for COVID and had been sick for some time but did recover. Several weeks later, the child had another fever and some other symptoms. Since it had been said that you could remain COVID-positive for several months after having the virus and this child had already been sick from it those several weeks earlier, the hospital probably figured her illness was associated with that same illness or maybe assumed the child was battling something less threatening than COVID since any illness other than that virus at the time seemed to rarely be considered serious. This was a time I could not rationalize people's actions. I am only telling this story as I heard it, and it did give me more perspective on how off-track our society had become. The child was sent home, and when her condition continued to deteriorate, her mom brought her back to the hospital, hoping for some kind of answers and help as she could tell something was very wrong and she knew she did not have much more time. The child did have another infection, and it did end up getting much worse because it was not treated sooner, and now there was a need for aggressive and immediate treatment to save the child's life. Could it be that if her mom did not remain diligent and a solid advocate for her kid, responding to her maternal instincts, the child could have died? It would have been God's choice to take the life, but he allowed there to be power through maternal intervention, supporting storge and the concept of relativity. One thing about COVID that I saw firsthand was that it could seem like the person was okay and recovered but then could have a relapse and become very sick again or possibly pick up another infection that was exacerbated by recently having COVID. It was thought that this "weakness" in the immune system meant that the person was still not out of the woods, even when showing improvement, and should take measures to boost the immune system during that time to prevent more illness. After contracting any illness, our body's immune system is busy battling and can get distracted or just remain weak for some time as the body completely heals. We should have used this understanding better when seeing patients. There seemed to be an increase in type 1 and 2 diabetes, GI problems, and bleeding issues that may have resulted several months after a COVID infection or stayed as an ongoing issue. COVID seemed to attack a particular organ in the body and then cause serious issues for the patient. It was even said to increase estrogen levels in women during the infection, and then when the levels drop quickly after the illness, it would cause hair loss and other issues with the hormone shift. It seemed that these symptoms could last for upward of six months and even longer. Once the mRNA was factored in, later, it was thought that some people who had these COVID symptoms never recovered from them and stayed ill or with chronic infections or symptoms indefinitely because the body continued to cycle through the illness and weakened immune system as they continued getting boosters or whose bodies were overwhelmed by all the shedding. The adverse effects were said to follow whatever you were genetically predisposed to. I loved talking to people who saw this too, and it was nice to know other people were seeing things and being honest about what was seemingly going on.

Chapter 6

Surviving COVID and Trusting God to Be the Judge

Some agencies refused to use ivermectin or hydroxychloroquine to treat patients, even though these drugs seemed to have some good results battling the disease. I made sure to get a prescription filled to have these drugs on hand in case I needed to use them to battle the illness. I had people call me, since they knew I was an advocate for good health, and they would tell me how they were successful with finding treatment for battling COVID. Some people also included monoclonal antibodies, but these were only available to people who knew how or where to get these treatments because medical representatives were not making this information readily available to everyone. Why the big secret? The screening process was difficult, and the window of opportunity was small to be able to receive the antibodies. Even after a doctor in my area was being looked at for being open and honest about her findings concerning the vaccine, and needing to fight for her license to practice, was still working to provide preventative treatment. They even called me after my prescription was expired and asked if I wanted to have a refill even though ivermectin was said to be impossible to get and even being "destroyed" before it could be delivered to those who ordered it. I had no problem getting it, and the doctor stayed in contact with me for future treatment needs. I know God protected those who channeled truth. There were so many lies about treatments that worked, and people who had facts were called the liars. People were hospitalized and were only being treated with drugs that did not seem to work as well or as fast or even at all, but once they were in the hospital, they felt helpless to get needed meds from their family members. People reached out to me, concerned for their sick family members as they knew there were other options available that were just not being looked at. I wonder how many stories can be told of a family member bringing their loved one a milkshake spiked with ivermectin, and they made a remarkable turnaround and the staff caring for the patient thought it was the regime the hospital was using that finally cured the patient.

My dad had an interesting situation. He called his medical doctor to get a prescription for ivermectin to have on hand in case he ever got COVID. He made an appointment and went into the office requesting this prescription, and the nurse was confused. She said she saw on the news that this drug was only for horses. When he got called back to his room, he asked the doctor if he knew about ivermectin. The doctor said he did and would prescribe it to him but that he had to be discreet because the doctor said he would be targeted if those above him knew he prescribed it for COVID. The doctor said he believed in the drug and said that if my dad ever did get COVID, ivermectin would need to be taken right away and would show results. It would be working well, and within five days from getting infected, he would be getting better. The doctor said he was not allowed to show that he was treating COVID with ivermectin, but if he could explain he was just treating another condition with the drug, then he would not get into trouble prescribing it to my dad. We could only assume that those in higher leadership positions did not want people getting better from COVID. They wanted control. They wanted only the use of certain drugs being used as treatment like the one that was causing people to go into kidney failure but did not cure COVID infections. Hospitals were using this drug even though patients were dying after having COVID, but dying from multi-organ failure, possibly related to the kidney-toxic drugs. Some people listen to everything people say. Some people believe there is hope for their loved one even though the hospital says there is nothing left to do but remove life support and let their loved one die. Some people, it was reported, would move their loved one to another facility where other methods were tried, and they made a full recovery, even though they were told there was no hope and to let go. Some doctors were reportedly marking deaths as COVID, regardless of the real cause of death, and some were doing it the way they were trained in medicine, marking down what the actual cause of death was. Hospitals were said to get financial support for COVID deaths. If lots of people were dying of multi-organ failure, that would raise questions. Was the person mishandled or treated inappropriately? Was it a lack of treatment that let the illness just take over a person who could have fought it with proper meds? Was it a toxic drug that was given that did not fight COVID but did attack the patient's organs, so they died with COVID, not of COVID? It was reported that hospitals were getting funded for putting patients on ventilators too. Suddenly, more and more people were put on them. Judas Iscariots were being birthed all over the place. One nurse, who I heard of, in my area said she had to leave her hospital because they were putting people on ventilators when it was not indicated, assuming it was so the hospital could gain financially, and then they could not get them weaned off. She could not, with a clear conscience, keep working there. Ventilators were then said to be needed. Before long, there was a shortage. The word was that there was a shortage because COVID was so bad and everyone should be more afraid. What about the possibility that what we were hearing was true, that hospitals were overusing vents to get more money for patients in their care and not treating them properly so they would get better without ventilator use or better without even needing to be admitted.

Later, after the "vaccine" came out, a nurse I knew put on social media that anyone who did not get vaccinated should not get a ventilator if they get sick with COVID, because they were irresponsible and did not deserve to be on a ventilator. So now there was shaming for not seeing things one way. This nurse didn't get in trouble for violating the code of ethics; she advanced her license and became a leader in the field. It was intense, and I could not believe how this illness just flipped the world upside down. What kind of nurse would shame people for planning about their health and deciding what was appropriate for them? Where was the autonomy and respect for human life?

I had a friend who told me she was offered money to pay for her dad's funeral if the doctor would put COVID on the death certificate. People were coming out about how doctors and nurses were bullied into not reporting deaths and adverse effects from the vaccines just like COVID was put on death certificates when the patient had other morbidities that were believed to have been the actual cause of their death. If someone had a positive COVID test, the coroner would allow the doctor to say that the patient died of COVID, and many doctors wanted to have this kind of sway. Maybe they got more money for the patients they cared for who had the virus. The same administration that approved the medicine that was thought to cause renal failure and death in patients whom it was used on to supposedly treat COVID was now approving the mRNA.

I later found out that the dosage that the doctor gave my dad was not the right dosage since ivermectin is weight-based. This useless prescription was kept in my dad's cabinet serving as a believed tool to fight COVID if he needed it. I never checked his prescription. It was not until he came down with COVID symptoms, had a positive test, and was sick after being exposed to the virus that I found out what this prescription was. I asked him what dosage the doctor gave him, and when he told me, I was immediately shocked. He was on his deathbed and could not even walk but to the bathroom and back to bed. He had brain fog, disorientation, extreme nausea, a headache that was so painful he wanted to die, and said he was never sicker in his life. By now he had been sick for a while, and I knew he was in the vortex of the storm. He had been taking the ivermectin prescribed by his doctor, and there was no improvement in his symptoms. He was disappointed, and I was confused because I knew the medicine worked, and now he was too sick to even fight. Thank God I thought to ask him what the dosage was. I never imagined the doctor would be dishonest. My dad told me some ridiculous dosage, and I told him that number was way off. It was not a therapeutic dose of ivermectin, and this doctor tricked him into believing this drug would save him if he took it during a COVID infection. My dad could have died waiting for that drug to start working! My family acted quick and got him the correct dosage from another doctor, someone I trusted, and soon after taking the right dosage of ivermectin and getting nursed back to health by his family, he quickly turned the corner and made a full recovery, except for the lasting weak taste symptom, which stayed for a while, he had no lasting effects. This was by the grace of God.

    The doctor who initially gave him the prescription for ivermectin was evil and did not treat my dad with respect, admitting that it was because my dad did not get the COVID vaccine. He was punishing him for that decision by way of how he treated him. I had spoken to this man on the phone and was told by him in a later conversation that my parents did not want to get vaccinated and implied that if they were sick, that was why, and it was their fault. That doctor would not help them but only steered them to the hospital, which I knew was a death sentence. Therefore, the doctor discriminated against him and breached his oath as a doctor. He pretended to help by giving him the right drug but not the right strength. This doctor wrote a prescription and gave my dad a false sense of security by giving him a drug at a strength that would not have been effective even for a small child. He should have his license taken away. He was also responsible for ignoring my mom when she had requested help from him while on her deathbed. He refused to help her because she chose not to get vaccinated. He had also said earlier in her treatment process that it was her fault that she was sick because she abused alcohol, so she deserved to be in the condition she was in. He did not care that she had symptoms of things he could treat to help her in her condition and ease her pain and discomfort at the end. He decided he was judge. He decided he would take God's place and decided who he would treat right and who he would punish under his license. He believed he had this power. My mom's medical team denied her a promised liver transplant after she changed her life and found a donor in my sister, but since she would not get vaccinated, they canceled the plans. They cared about business and reputation. They were freelancing their authority as medical professionals instead of acknowledging the truth that medicine is not an exact science and they do operate under God who is supreme. They did not act in honor. They did not acknowledge truth or even honor their simple oaths and promises made to patients. This is another pandemic nationwide. She had liver disease and coronary artery disease among some other health problems and did pass away after she was refused care and established plan of care was not followed through by the very popular and nationally recognized medical organization whose care she was under. My mom tells a story even while her body is asleep, and I listen. According to her death certificate by the coroner, she died of her chronic health conditions including end-stage liver disease and coronary artery disease. Her doctor and her medical team only cared about the bottom line. They do not care about people. They do not have what it takes, the faith, the guts, the honor, and courage to truly help people. They are cowards. She ended up dying without help from her medical team, and although God is the author of life and death, I know this doctor and the team of people involved all the way up and down the chain are responsible for violating ethics, oaths, and God himself by not extending their hand to my mom, their patient, when she needed them. They are liars and frauds, and my mom's blood is on their hands, but still, they continue to practice today as "medical professionals" although this is not who they are. They should be in jail, and this is one very big reason I do not trust all doctors or the medical field. I told my parents to leave their primary care doctor years before this, but they were loyal to him because they had been going to him for so long and trusted him. They wanted to give him good business. Loyalty was not reciprocated to my parents. If doctors do not have good character, they might as well get their license from a Cracker Jack box. This man was very good at scheduling lots of appointments for my mom and charging her insurance. Her health condition was good profit for him, but was the money he made worth my mom's life? I forgive these people because God says so. I would not do what they did to my mom and punish them forever for wrongdoing. I forgive them. However, these medical professionals in these leadership positions need to want to change or should not be given the privilege to serve others in this capacity. Their actions were malicious and violent, yet they go unpunished. They need to admit they were wrong, or they will be judged by God, and this would be a righteous judgment for them. A doctor who practices medicine without a good heart is as useful as a toilet that doesn't flush.

We could have taken this man to court along with the huge "successful" hospital that chose to hold back care to my mom when she needed it to live, but we chose to leave them to God because he has enough justice for us all. My mom is still safe with God as she was her whole life; nothing changed for her in that way, which is the silver lining. She grew closer to God while the medical field took advantage of her and used her for the profit of money, stringing her along to do "good business." This evil is going on across our whole country. It is a pandemic we refuse to cure. My mom loved these people, and she would forgive them even now. She taught me well, and I will continue to honor her name. We did find out later that some people who had gotten vaccinated and then got organ transplants were rejecting their new organs. This would make perfect sense if you understand the mRNA and how it works. My mom made a good decision, and I am proud of her still today. My mom's story made it to national news as she was finally cleared and ready for liver transplant surgery after she and my sister embarked on an extensive and rigorous journey of testing, hard work, medical planning, and commitment—only to be suddenly denied the life-saving surgery when they both refused to take the newly mandated COVID injection. My mom tried, even going on the national news, to get help to have this long-awaited surgery and to fight for herself, even her life. No one came to her rescue, and the hospital overlooked her cry for help. She died reportedly due to her failing health, which included end-stage liver disease shortly after the liver transplant surgery plan was canceled. This should outrage Americans, and those responsible for withholding treatment should be held accountable for this crime along with those spreading malicious ideology concerning the COVID injections. The medical field is fraudulent, and this negligent behavior and breach of ethics in medicine needs to be addressed.

Me and my dad fighting for medical freedom at Washington D.C. in 2022 after my mom faced medical and religious discrimination, was refused care and promised treatment, and later died.

Chapter 7

Informed Consent

The problem I see in medicine is that people depend on things, facilities, protocols, and algorithms instead of faith and facts. The patients remind me to have faith, and through those who cannot speak, I learned to listen in other ways, which is powerful in exposing truth. One day, while working on the maternity unit during COVID pandemic when the mask protocol was still in use, I had to run to the NICU for something. When I got to the counter, I was met by a nurse who said, "Hey! I know you! You're a nurse on the mom and baby unit! You saved me! I knew I would never forget your face. Even with the mask on, I know it is you." She continued telling her story, and I listened. I just looked at her as she talked, and my memory was jogged. She said, "I was there on your unit, and I began hemorrhaging the day after my baby was born. There was blood everywhere, and I was in so much pain. I thought I was dying. The nurse could not figure out what was wrong. You came in to help and came to my bedside. You looked at me and knew exactly what to do. You pushed on my abdomen so hard I thought it was going down through to my back. The pain was so intense, but then a huge clot came out, and immediately, the pain and bleeding stopped. You saved my life that day. I was immediately better. I knew I would never forget you. Thank you so much! My daughter is eighteen months old now, and I know I wouldn't be here today without you."

    I remembered her story. I was stunned and overwhelmed with what she was saying. I told her it was nice to hear her story and about her daughter growing up too. This was God in me. This is the power that goes out from nurses who live by faith and do things they learned through experience and good teaching from experienced nurses. This is the type of thing that the hospital I am at does not value. I was so humbled that day and floated back to my unit, light on my feet as I knew God was the reason I did anything good for people, and to have someone else see him in me and be able to speak about it with their own mouth was such a miracle. I was so thankful and forever grateful for her story and all that God proved to do for others through faith.

Some other stories did not have the same ending as people didn't choose to live by faith. I heard a story about a baby that died in the second trimester, and a nurse who made note about how the mother had gotten the second dose of the COVID vaccine just a week prior to the death of the child. The mother had a headache and nausea for a week after the shot, and at that time, once the baby stopped moving, she went into the office and found out the baby had died. The doctor noted that it must have been from some kind of congenital abnormality that was unidentified even though the blood work done earlier showed the patient to have a normal pregnancy for the most part and there were no signs of congenital abnormalities. I do not know if the doctor ever reported the incident, but he made no mention of the possibility of it being caused by the mRNA when talking to the mother, according to information, even when she asked if the death of her baby could be her fault. Could the shot have caused the death of the baby? Why were doctors not willing to answer this question? It seemed that informed consent was going out the window. When someone puts something in their body, they have a right to know what could happen as a result. I believe this woman was asking if the shot could have affected her unborn baby and could be responsible for the child's death. The medical field failed this woman and many women, men, and children all over the world by simply not giving all the facts that were available.

God is the taker of life, but our actions are of importance and relative to others. None of us are perfect, and we certainly never know it all, but what we do know we are responsible for sharing as medical professionals, and this is when you decide to display integrity or not. The baby died, and it went "unexplained." God is sovereign. He takes life. This mother could not have taken the life of her child even if she tried. She does not have power to take life. God had to be involved here to allow it, but our actions do carry accountability. For instance, we as humans would be accountable for the act of murder if that act was committed and God decided to take the life, but our act of murder does not take the life. God takes it. The act is already sin, even as a thought in our minds, and before the action even takes place, we are guilty of sin. It is always God's decision to give and take life, but we as parents need to understand that our decisions can and do impact our kids and that we are held accountable as parents under God for decisions we make. It is all relative. Even our very thought processes are important and must be paid attention to. He is a forgiving God if we ask, and we need to understand these mechanics, and we need to be careful of the decisions we make in life as they do have an effect. This concept needs to be understood by coaches and leaders in our country because we are all held accountable for what we are encouraging others to do. What the sports world is doing—encouraging young women to be involved in a popularity contest on the court and encouraging them to disrespect and dishonor their bodies in ways that will generate profit for the organizations—is a form of abuse and extortion. It's happening at lower levels and all the way to the top. Have you noticed the difference in the photos taken for sports, encouraging kids to worship themselves instead of just being proud to be an athlete or someone of good character? You must look "cool" now in the pictures, and this is gearing the kids up for the bigger levels where the "cooler" they look, the better, because image is king. They will need to compete with how the body looks instead of the condition of the heart. The image preferred does not reflect any good attributes of the heart but instead shows someone who is a slave to this world and all it offers. Even self-care is worshipped in this country to make women into sex symbols or physical idols. The outside shell of a person, their image and witness, is important because the body is to be recognized as a "temple" of God. What you want to be recognized as on the inside will be seen in how you dress, act, and present your body on the outside. You should appear "holy and blameless" if this is what you hope to become in God's eyes.

There is a problem in our country, and it is growing bigger by the minute. Why are coaches encouraging kids to be fans of these idols on social media who call themselves athletes, leaders, and self-care gurus who are not good role models and whose actions and appearance represent the prince of the air? Coaches should be protecting our kids. Sports programs should be authentic in leadership principles. We have been invaded by impostors. We are all parents by grace, and we all need to know that. We should be encouraged to protect our kids and should know the medical risks we take when we are given choices and offered services in society. Likewise, you should know what you're up against when you allow your kids to indulge in social media and worldly organizations that are looking to gain from your kids while hurting them. I understand the issue is that parents want their kids to be able to be involved and to have the opportunity to play honorable sports, to have coaches they trust, programs that teach good morals, and to have good health and doctors who care. I want these too. However, we must stop accepting what is offered to us when it is unhealthy. Take a stand for your kids. Require the bar to be raised. This must be required of yourself too, but God promises not to let you down. There is a better quality of life that our nation is missing out on. More and more people started to come out and speak about other situations where much death and adverse effects were believed to be caused by the COVID vaccine, but doctors were not reporting the instances, so the numbers and statistics were inaccurate. This was looked at to expose the truth in a movement called ProjectVeritas.com. Nurses and doctors who were honest wanted to blow the whistle on the corruption. I hope athletes and medical professionals will turn the tide and start standing up to be true role models.

It was thought that whatever you were genetically predisposed to is how your disease and symptoms would present after you got the mRNA or COVID. It was said they could also awaken a dormant virus in your body. If you had a dormant virus in your body such as West Nile or mono, you were more susceptible to these infections, and they could and did cause severe illness in people. It was thought the mRNA wakened these viruses that were dormant in the body from a prior infection that the person either knew or did not know they had. You could have had a prior infection and not known it because the body protected you by way of your natural immunity. In cases like mono and West Nile, the virus, which may have never made you sick at the time it entered your body, lay dormant. If the mRNA awakened the virus, it could then be so severe that it would affect the neurologic system, which debilitated its victims for long periods of time or even permanently. Some people just chalked it up to an outbreak somewhere and blamed a random mosquito that must have found them when they were not looking, but why didn't they look at the facts about the shot? Other people had their hearts affected or had seizures that developed after getting the shot but maybe attributed it to a coincidence. Some people developed kidney disease, and many people developed bleeding, clotting issues, and cardiac dysfunction after receiving the mRNA. Some people were not seemingly affected at all because there were supposedly placebos going out as well.

Unfortunately, some kids and adults were not properly taken care of, and many did die or have major illness that could have possibly been prevented. If God ever uses us to help him heal another, we should consider it a gift of grace that we could be used for such a thing, whether it is through advice, treatment, training, or another act. God just desires a relationship with us, and this is why he uses us to further his kingdom through caring for others through mind, body, and spirit. He does not actually need our help but wants the relationship. I am only sharing these stories to help us as people to act better and to be diligent to see how we can better serve and see others. We do have power to respond to people to make an impact on their lives for better or worse, and we should work to make their lives better, not worse. The way the world is going, our oaths and commitment to excellence do not matter to some as people are breaching the code of ethics every day and going without punishment. People were not and are not getting taken care of and for no acceptable reason. Organizations were worried about losing money, and profit was put above people. As a parent, I can say I appreciate those who use their own minds and the spirt of God to lead them as they take care of their kids and families well, especially during the pandemic. I also appreciated the people including medical staff and those in the community who did act with good heart and exercised faith as they jumped through hoops and moved around red tape to make sure they still loved others as God does and were willing to give good treatment and advice to others, no matter the cost. These people stood out to me. I am thankful there was a doctor who was willing to prescribe ivermectin; otherwise, my dad may have not recovered from his COVID symptoms. God is the author of life and death, but people who intervene on behalf of patients do make the difference, and these people are blessed and are given power through grace to make things happen. Miracles still happen today. People who were negatively affected need to stand up and admit the truth. Those who spoke truth, during this time, motivated me. I tried hard to forge ahead inspired by these people and their stories.

Chapter 8

America the Beautiful

What makes America different from other countries is the fact that we network and we raise up men and women who work in factories, organizations, and at all different levels. We teach trades and have different jobs of service, and all these jobs and people work together to make the whole. America has become who we are because we understand that everyone has different talents that they bring to the table, which positively influences others and can complement the work of their neighbor. Allowing everyone to thrive in their own way is what helps our country to communicate through so many different channels and avenues of development and to invite the creativity of so many diverse, open-minded people. This is why we have the best intel and machinery and strategies in our military. It is why we have been so successful over the years and why other countries envy us. Other countries have too much control over their people, and it is their downfall. They tell them what to do instead of inspiring learning and reasoning, supporting autonomy and the process of people figuring things out for themselves. In this process, transformational leadership can be experienced, and this is valuable to our country in raising up powerful men and women. This very concept is under attack in America and is a pandemic in and of itself.

The workout program of jump stretch is effective to inspire people to strive even through hard times by way of tough workouts of mind, body, and spirit. This program helps to battle against this pandemic to resuscitate the heart of a lion in athletics and everyday life. The concept of transformational leadership develops the link between questions and answers and aids in new creations, ideas, and projects that lead to success in a country that has so much freedom to grow potential. By having too much control, barriers develop, and it minimizes the amount of production and weakens the infrastructure of the country altogether. By giving people freedom to thrive in their own organic ways, they branch off and can start new growth of success in others, and the process continues. We are moving away from this tolerating crooked organizations who are giving people platforms to promote the weak mindset of self-worship. Our country cannot thrive with people in leadership positions who only care about themselves. We need to stop putting these people in top executive positions or in positions to negatively influence our youth in sports and school.

 I once had a conversation with someone who told me to imagine what would happen if a group of talented Americans were sent to another country to establish a clean and sanitary water system but did not complete the mission by investing in the execution of operations with locals before leaving. If we fund the project, build a system, and are successful but never teach the minds of the people using the system how to maintain it or manufacture the necessary parts to sustain it, how long will it last? If we withdraw ourselves from the country after this project was seemingly completed, it will only last so long because we only shared the physical hardware and offered the borrowing of mind power; we never influenced the long-term change by investing in the minds and hardware of the people who remain. This means we keep the greatest gift to ourselves and keep people dependent on us for their success, and this would not support authentic leadership.

 During COVID pandemic, we were taught to just do it and to not ask any questions. We were given money that we would suffer for later. Some people provided service, while others worshipped self and became rich during the time, taking for themselves. This is not the American way. It seemed like we forgot who we were, or maybe we were adopting other countries' strategies instead of having regard for our own teaching on authentic leadership principles. I was now impressed with those who were willing to go to work even when there was the option and encouragement to stay home. This was an honorable decision, but even this only means we were doing our simple duty. Going to work and providing a service will not make anyone righteous because only God can do that, but faith without deeds is dead, so it was reassuring in some ways to see faith being practiced and kept alive by some, and I was encouraged by it. Inspiring others to do it would be the work of true leaders and would be to reach another level. How could this be done? People say they live by faith, but faith is an exercise. Talking about having faith and having it are different. To teach our youth to only focus on their bodies, offering a devaluing system that puts themselves out to the world in ways that are not beneficial to themselves or others causes harm in so many ways. It is relative to the corruption our country has seen and is yet another pandemic that is being hugely overlooked.

God did not tell us to stay home. He tells us to go out into the world because he inspires others through us. One thing that was a positive result from COVID was the fact that from the shutdowns came people who realized they no longer wanted what big businesses and corporations had to offer, and they in turn opened their own business and branched out in positive, productive, and beneficial ways they never otherwise would have. Shutdowns were supporting the great resignation. Big business had corrupted itself to the point of expecting nonsense from employees, forcing them to push to impress the leaders of their companies but never seeming to do so. The workers were trying so hard but found themselves disappointed after running in an endless hamster wheel, which ultimately led to burnout. I saw this firsthand as a nurse. The greed from those at the top who were overworking and underpaying employees eventually caused massive numbers of workers across America to resign from their jobs.

One day, at the beginning of the shutdowns, as I cleaned my kitchen, I began to wonder how I would manage to buy food since the stores were empty. I decided not to worry but, instead, to clean the fridge out and somehow knew I would be able to put food in it. That very moment, as I was on the floor cleaning the fridge, my dad walked into my house, and I looked up at him as he stood in the doorway with a twenty-pound box of fish and some other food items, and I thought, *Wow, God, that was fast!* I did not even have the fridge cleaned yet, and there was the food. It makes me laugh thinking about all that we worry about when God already has what we need in life and has a plan in place. My dad just looked at me, and I looked up at him as he said, "Hey, you guys need some food? They had this fish on sale at the store. I could not pass it up, and I figured you guys could use it." Everyone was stocking up on "survival food," which I guess was chicken and beef, and maybe fish does not fall into the category of survival food? I do not know. I was not trying to figure out the details involved in the panicked shoppers' mind, but I know my family loves fish, and this was enough for a few meals, so I was so thankful. That was before my mom died, and she was being admitted again into the hospital for some treatments for her liver disease, and my dad was looking for a way to get rid of some of the food he had in his fridge since he would not be cooking for my mom for a while. He stayed at the clinic and slept many nights in his car just to be close to my mom when they would not let him in to see her, so he ate light on the go while she was in the hospital. He never complained. They had ways of helping my mom to have a better quality of life, but they, instead, wanted to study her and take her insurance payments whenever she had a flare-up. She was used and abused as a patient as so many people are. This was a hard time for my family, but we battled through, and we learned so much.

When I did finally get to the grocery store, I was thankful for the experience of finding things that no one else wanted. When I first walked in and saw that the shelves were empty, it was strange and felt desolate, but after that feeling passed, I was left feeling like the glass was half full, not half empty and decided to teach the kids that this was an adventure. I pushed the buggy and muffled through my mask, "Come on, guys. Let us see what we can find." So since everyone bought out the eggs, chicken, and white rice, we bought salmon, shrimp, and brown rice. I also bought chicken tortellini. I had never cooked with chicken tortellini before, but I figured, why not try something new? When we got home with our groceries, I realized I had ingredients to maybe make a soup. I got creative and decided to make something delicious because being resourceful with the items I was able to get at the store was a challenge, and facing challenges was what I was built to do. I got out my big soup pot and added the chicken tortellini, brown rice, carrots, celery, broccoli, kidney beans, salt, pepper, parsley, basil, and chicken broth. I slow-boiled it until it was perfect, and of course, my family loved it! This experience taught me that sometimes it may seem like we got the lesser hand in life. Maybe we feel jaded or that we were not given as good a gift, talent, or resource as our neighbors, and that makes us feel like the only option is to fail or feel sorry for ourselves and make excuses for not trying hard. If you believe you need something that is not there, ask God. You must be willing to take paths you did not expect to take. Sometimes you may even feel like you are taking a step backward instead of forward, but in time if you stay connected to him, you will find your way to blessings. Be patient.

We are not vulnerable. We were not victims during COVID pandemic. We all have much potential and are all capable of living beautiful lives and being developed into God's beautiful masterpieces. If we do not have all we need, God can use others as seasoning to add flavor to what we will become in life, and this is the beauty I find in the diverse world around me. We are all different and are all good ingredients to add flavor to the world to spice it up and make it delicious. This reminds us of how God says he wants us to salt the earth. This was the concept I used when cooking during the pandemic, but it is also the concept I use in everyday living in the world of sports, school, and work. Season those lives around you to spice up their life and make it better without any excuse. Work to build others up and be a dynamic and a powerful resource to be used by God to season the people of earth. This concept is a key missing in leadership of big corporations, and this has caused many families to be in hardship, forcing our country to fold in on itself. Just like proteins that can fold into their pathologic forms and cause disease, we as people in our country can do the same. We are fighting against ourselves. We are a sick nation, plagued by our own system. Our country has allowed hospitals, sports organizations, and big businesses to imply that they have control over those they govern. We, as a society, let this go on, supporting and believing these groups when they say they promote inclusion but are the enemy, wolves in sheep's clothing, fueling the fire of hate. This has provided more room for self-pleasure and comfort. The corruption of big business overshadows our country.

Here is another meal I was able to put together out of the limited resources that were made available to me. Usually, noodles are a staple in our house, but you could not find a noodle anywhere after everyone panic-shopped, so I kept pushing my buggy around the store looking for a carb that caught my eye. I found organic black bean noodles. Since Sabria and I were intrigued anyway with all the positives we had recently learned surrounding the consumption of plant-based proteins, especially in relation to athletic conditioning and training, I decided this could be a good thing to try, and so I put them in the buggy. I enjoy all different types of food and encourage variety. I finished my shopping, and for dinner, I once again got creative. It may sound like I enjoy working in the kitchen, but I would rather be doing pretty much anything else. It takes much energy out of my life to put meals together that will do the right thing for my body and my family's bodies but also taste good. I do try to enjoy cooking because I must spend a lot of time in my life doing it, and that would be a lot of time to waste feeling sorry for myself or doing the job badly or not at all just because I do not want to do it. I try to find passion in cooking because it is an area of my life that I cannot get away from if I want to take good care of my family, so I decide how I am going to feel about it. Have you ever found yourselves in a place you did not want to be in but knew you had purpose there? This is how I look at cooking. Besides, it is while doing the most mundane activities in life that God speaks to me, and I love to listen while I work. This dish is so quick and simple but packed with nutrients and great for active people, like athletes. I took my largest pan and sautéed shrimp, cherry tomatoes, garlic, parsley, cumin, salt, and basil together with coconut oil. I topped the prepared black bean noodles boiled and drained then tossed with coconut oil, salt, pepper, garlic, and parsley with the sautéed shrimp mixture and again made a delicious and healthy meal that my family loved. In life, we sometimes do not like the way we look and would prefer to look this way or that. We want to maybe be good at one sport and strive to be the best at it but find we are better at another sport, and then we shift a little in that direction to better fit in. Sometimes we live most of our lives not knowing what we are good at and are always unsettled in our spirit, never seeming to find peace with who we are supposed to be. I learned even through these cooking experiences that you can have a beautiful life if you decide to find that what you have been given by God is beautiful and worth something. You need to have faith in what you have been given and know it is good, then you can share what you have with others, keeping America beautiful.

Chapter 9

Pressure On, Pressure Off

I met a particular family about seventeen years ago when I took care of a man whose kids were left with the decisions of end-of-life care. This experience allowed me to learn the benefit of a weathered attitude, although at the time I was still new to the idea. I only had hope that what I was experiencing was for the good. I now understand more of what I was learning then. I had taken care of this man a few times for an exacerbation of certain health problems that earned him a room on the critical care unit. He was on a ventilator and was now beginning his end-of-life journey as his organs were shutting down. I worked the evening shift at the time, and when I got to work on a particular day and received my assignment, I then sat down for report with the other nurses.

    That day the man's family had discussed their options and decided that it was time to let their dad go and to stop all care being done, as it became clear that his body was tired and there was nothing left that could be done to help him. We would only continue care that would keep him comfortable as he died. He was deteriorating, and they did not want him to suffer any longer in that condition. It became clear to the family that it was time to let him go. The decision was made right before I got to work, so my job was to relieve the day-turn nurse so she could go home, and then I would need to begin the process of shutting down all the machines of life support and making the man as comfortable as possible. This is the mechanical work. The real work was that I would be there alongside this man and his family as he passed on from this life on earth to the life lived in eternity.

As I felt my heart tug, I became stoic. I can picture myself even now walking down the hallway toward his room and hearing his daughter cry saying she did not want to let her dad go but knew it was time. "Oh, Dad," she said. Then she looked at me as tears of grief and desperation streamed down her face, and she muttered out those words I have heard so many times. "I do not know how you do what you do. I do not know how you do this job. I could never do it." I just looked at her, knowing this would be so tough on this family, and I was easily connected to them as the man reminded me of my own grandpa, my mom's dad. So I pictured these people as my family and thought of them as though they could be my mom and her siblings being in a similar situation. I was brought back to the time when my grandpa died of Lou Gehrig's disease and how my mom struggled to take care of her dad throughout his progressive illness and then ultimately had to say goodbye to him. I was young at the time, but I remember her being frantic when it finally happened. Even though death was imminent for my patient, his kids, just like my mom, were not ready to say goodbye. This was where this family was when I came into work that day. I had to redirect my thoughts to remain diligent and focused on my job as a nurse but also a friend and support to this family. I had other patients too, probably three others who were all critically ill, and nurses were expected to just move from one room to the next and do what needed done for all the patients individually. We seem like robots sometimes in how we can do this, but we are not, and for me, it all eventually catches up.

I kept my composure and walked down to the respiratory therapist's office and talked with her about the plan to make sure we were both on the same page. We both walked into the patient's room; she walked to the ventilator, and I went to the IV pump. I adjusted the pain medicine he was getting to keep him comfortable as we began shutting off the vent and removing the tubes from his body. These are the moments I feel God kneading me. Through my life, I feel like, it is pressure on, pressure off, pressure on, pressure off. It is like he is saying, "Tina, change. See me. Help these people. Do what

I made you to do." So it really felt like the pressure was on more than off because at every level of my life, I struggled. I was always in debt, chasing the kids around, begging my husband to be part of us, cleaning the house to no end, and then leaving that house and all the struggles there, to get into that hospital. I was there to help people to either struggle and fight to recover or to die being comforted as they walked across that bridge to the next life, and along with that came helping their families to say goodbye. I was really pressed all the time, only getting short breaks to recover and catch my breath at work and at home, but God told me to keep going, so I did. Sometimes our car would break down, and I would call my dad for a ride to that hospital, and he brought me. I had to fight even to get to that place that worked me to the bone, but I kept going, believing I made a difference. Sometimes he would stop there and bring me coffee. I still have the sleeve from a cup of coffee he bought me on one of my shifts, and I wrote the date on it. It is a keepsake, reminding me of tough days and a man who believed in me and loved me in times of need. I kept my workouts tough, and I did them religiously because it was therapeutic and a way to feel like I conquered something. No thinking was involved; for one moment in the day, I forced my mind to shut off during my workouts. Even with the kids running around and my chores stacked up, and sometimes it felt like it was not worth it to work out; but still, I believed it was, and it cleared my brain. I needed that hour to punch and kick and do push-ups and get out of breath, and for that time I did not think about sick people dying or all that waited for me throughout the day. I needed that hour or so of fighting, for me.

 I went into nursing school, originally to be an OB nurse and to help women the way I was helped when I had Sabria, my first child, when I was young and vulnerable and saw how the nurses loved me and gave me hope in a desperate time of my life. This was not God's complete plan for me, though. I got out of nursing school feeling confident and proud. I said to myself, "Here I go, onto maternity!" but the nursing field said something different. They said there were no maternity jobs available, so I had to go to medical-surgical nursing where most nurses get their foundation. I was upset at first and felt like I tricked myself into believing I could do something I would never get to do. Sometimes, though, God has us go down side streets before getting to the main road, like taking the scenic route. This is how he trains us. It is like practicing driving in parking lots and side streets before driving on the highway and in busy cities. It is a building process. I decided to trust God in this and fight through and get my feet wet in med-surg nursing as suggested and climb from there. It almost seemed like God was taking me to the city and highway first to drive, before the parking lots and side streets. It seemed backward, and I felt like I was not ready, but that is why I had to trust him. Instead of just getting my feet wet, it felt more like taking a plunge. Sometimes he does this to us to build our faith. He asks us to take steps or even leaps we do not feel prepared to take, but if we trust him, we can do these things because he always gives us what we need.

 I started out in a nursing home as an RN supervisor, and after realizing how short-staffed they keep things there, at least where I was, I could not stand it and had to leave. I saw people mistreated for self-profit twenty years ago, and it continues today. I was trained in acute care mostly, so this was where I was a better fit. Thankfully, during the time I was hoping to leave the nursing home, a young man in the rehab department said that I was young and I needed to get out of there and get some good experience. He told me of a critical care floor in a hospital near us that had a great manager, and he gave me her number. He said to call her and to give her his name and said that he referred me. He was an LPN there on that unit before they decided to cut the LPNs from the hospital. He said that usually people need to work up to being on that floor, but he would put in a good word for me. I did what he told me, and I got hired. I really believed at that point that God had a real good sense of humor for allowing me to go down this path, a path I did not choose directly but ended up being thankful for. This was where I remained for four years, and I got a view of life from a different angle, and I chose to appreciate the lessons. I also got a good foundation in nursing, and this experience could never have been taught to me. I had to be in the moments that gave me a raw talent for the job. It gave me intuition, wisdom, and instinct as a nurse. I learned how to troubleshoot and to critically think. I did not know the kind of experiences I would have and how God would knead me there, but then again, if I knew, I probably would not have been willing to go. God does not reveal all his plans to us right away. He gives us just enough to get going, to take that step.

The manager who hired me was the best boss I ever knew. She eventually moved on to a bigger facility, but I learned good leadership skills from her. She cared. I never forgot that beautiful family and how God used me to help them say goodbye. Back in those days, nurses were better appreciated as people. The corporation allowed nurses to work different shifts as they needed to, to take care of their own family. I worked eight-hour shifts back then. I also worked sixteen-hour shifts, but I chose this when it was appropriate for me. Times have changed, and now nurses do not have the same flexibility. Twelve-hour shifts are mandatory in most facilities. If a nurse chooses this and it works well for their family, this should be considered, but to have a corporation force these long shifts on nurses is one reason many nurses leave the field. Some facilities require more college, which is not necessary and not always beneficial to nurses as their time and energy is taken from their families. Some days a twelve-hour shift is appropriate, but many days it is not, and a nurse should have that choice. You can't teach experience, and I do believe people at the corporate level, unfortunately, move up the chain prematurely and are not qualified to be in leadership positions.

My mom was proud of my nursing school graduation picture from 2003. She helped me to respect the pin and cap by teaching me to put people over profit and to keep this as my principle.

Chapter 10

What Am I Doing Here?

When I was just beginning my career and new to the critical care unit, which will take me back about seventeen years, I remember asking myself the question, What am I doing here? One day I went into work and had received a patient that day in my assignment who was recently transferred from surgical intensive, another trauma victim. He was not settled on our unit yet, and the transfer did not go as well as hoped. This was a young man, even younger than I was at the time, and I was about twenty-two years old, just starting out in my career. I received report on the patient and was astonished to hear of this young man's story. Apparently, he had gotten a job as a delivery boy for a furniture company. One day he had ventured out as normal to make a delivery to a house in the country. It had been raining that day, which made a mess of the ground, and although he had been trained to get out of his truck on the grass side of the street to be safe and careful to avoid injury from cars passing him on the street, he decided this would be too much of a mess. I am sure he did not realize the seriousness of his decision that day. He chose to ignore his training and do what seemed to make better sense. There was a large puddle on the grass side of the street, so to avoid this, he decided to get out of his truck on the street side. He was then struck by a semitruck that he did not see coming. His body was thrown and destroyed by the impact, and this was how I encountered this young man and met him for the first time.

I did not expect to become a trauma nurse, but this was where God had me, taking care of people and families after trauma of all kinds. I wanted to be a maternity nurse, so I did often ask myself the question, What am I doing here? Nevertheless, I continued in the world of medical-surgical nursing and loved people as God told me to, never knowing how long he would keep me doing this. I entered this boy's room bewildered. He was a handsome boy, with what could have been a whole life ahead of him. Even though he was just barely younger than me, my motherly instincts came alive as I had a daughter and was pregnant with my son at the time. This young man was just starting out in life, trying to make a little money by being responsible to have a job. I am sure he had no idea that one little mistake on the job would end all of that. As I looked at his body and could see the damage done, I had to shake my head no, no, no. *How could this be*, I thought. *This is so bad. His poor mother must be devastated beyond imagination.* He had been down in ICU for long enough that his hands and feet were beginning to curl, and he had some rigidity in his whole body. He could not breath on his own or regulate temperature, which told me of his extensive brain damage. Whenever we turned him or really moved him at all, he would tremble, and as his lungs sensed the congestion, this would cause him to "buck the vent," setting off alarms as his body attempted to do something it no longer could do but wanted to do. As I stood at his bedside, scanning his body from the top of his head to the bottom of his toes, I could not help myself from imagining what he looked like before the accident, what his hobbies were, what his voice sounded like, and if he had siblings who loved him. His name was perfectly picked by someone who loved him, and I was humbled to be with him at that moment, having to be the one to survey his situation and to act and move in love for him at that most difficult time. I just decided to treat him with respect and dignity and to be a fighter alongside him to give him the best chance to come out of this for his sake and for the sake of his loved ones who held out hope for their son, brother, friend, cousin, or maybe nephew. I did not know this boy or his family; I had never met them. I was able, though, to imagine he was special to many people. They could not be there with him, but I was there. His body was in such poor condition as a result of the injuries he sustained, and from the report I got and from the assessment I made as his nurse, I knew what all this meant. He was there in that bed physically, but his mind was in another world, and he was fighting for his life. He told me a story from his bed, even with no voice. The other nurse and I were desperately trying to stabilize him on our unit on that day, and from a medical standpoint, it was obvious that his youth was the only reason he had held out this long. His body was just deteriorating so fast. If God's plan was to keep him here on earth, I had no doubt that would have happened. But I would do all I could to help him until the end. The family still wanted every effort made to save his life, but his body was shutting down. As the ICU did get him to a point where they believed he could be transferred to us, his body had used up all its reserve. This was the time that his body was letting us know it was finished fighting. His brain was so damaged that it was just responding in ways that told us how severe of a situation this was, and we knew that soon, after every effort was made, the body would completely shut down. He was only on our unit for a short time before we transferred him back to the ICU. I prayed for a miracle for this boy as we quickly unhooked him from everything and had our team of nurses work together as one to get him hooked up to the portable heart monitor, and the bed unplugged while respiratory maintained his airway. We rushed down the hall, and as we passed the nurses' station, someone handed me the emergency medicine transport box on our way back to ICU in hopes that something more could be done to help him.

I began to feel small in the situation, but God had this boy in his hands. I found out that shortly after his trip back to ICU, the boy's family, after realizing all efforts were exhausted and there was nothing more to do, made the decision to take him off life support. I am sure his parents never made a harder decision, but for their son, it was what they needed to do to love him.

I never forgot this young man. I remember what room he was in, the nurses who were involved, the emotions I had, and the love I gave at the bedside; and this is what I focus on. Families saw us nurses as tough and unbreakable. But I saw the real us. We had to be tough for them so we could complete our mission and continue fighting and battling for their loved one and to see things emerging and act on them, even when we were busy. We chose to watch for the signs with each patient to know when and how we could do better for them. We chose to be an advocate for the patient since we were the ones with eyes on them. It was our duty. The doctors needed us to make good decisions concerning their patients when they were not there. We chose to spend time, even when we did not have it, to address matters when we could, in hopes of making a difference. We chose to listen to the family as they poured their hearts out about how this was not the loved one they once knew and how the patient in the bed was not always that way. We would listen to all the wonderful stories they had with their loved one from better days, before they were in this condition, in this bed, and in this place. We knew. We loved them where they were but also appreciated who we heard they were before. I would go into the break room to find one of the nurses losing it and crying over whatever they had going on with their patient when it just became too much for them to bear. We helped each other realize that it was important to remain strong for our patients and their families but that there was a time to cry and handle those emotions when we could, in private. Sometimes I would cry in the car, once I left work, or I would wait till I got home, and I would just cry out and clean out all those feelings in the shower. Sometimes I would dream about my patients and their families in my sleep, and God kept me connected to them and to reality in this way. These situations helped me to look at life differently and to be humble, thankful, kind, and understanding.

I had my own family at home to raise and to take care of, and I did bring my work home with me. Some people may think this is wrong, but I prayed for everyone I could and always asked God why. Why was this family going through this? Why did this patient have to suffer? It is important to ask why. This is the relationship part of us and God. He is not just a figment of our imagination. He should be our friend, our counselor, our tower of refuge and strength. I never get too tired to continue my missions with God because he preserves me. He keeps me able to see that the why is bigger than me. There are so many reasons that people go through things, and these experiences shape and mold all of us if we let them. Some patients wake up from comas and devastating injuries, and some do not, and while we do not always know what the result of our efforts will be, we need to treat all patients with dignity and respect. We should know that sometimes people do wake up from their comas and confirm that they did hear what was being said while they were asleep, telling us that they were somewhat aware of their surroundings, just unable to respond to us. While we do not always understand why things happen, we must believe that God has a plan, and we need to trust that he knows what is best.

These are the situations that built me and trained me to love my kids, my husband, family members, friends, and patients. My marriage was hard. My life was hard, but I remained hopeful through storms because I believed my efforts were blessed by God. Although I felt small at the bedside, God helped me realize I was made strong by him within me and that I should do all I could to help people in any way I could and that my efforts did matter no matter what the outcome would end up being. He oversaw the outcome, and I was responsible to walk in faith on the missions he put me on. It was faith that drove me because, of course, many times I did not see any worth in trying to make a difference. I just had to believe that God had a plan to make a change because there was power where I was and in what I was doing. This was him kneading me like dough and helping me find worth, a voice, and a purpose.

This was how I could not stay quiet after my Sabria got hurt at West Point, tearing her ACL in freshman year. I had to push for change and to be an advocate when I saw a chance to make a difference and a reason to try and promote change in my domain. I did not know ten years earlier that I would need these experiences with these patients to help me be strong for my daughter and to hear her cries for help. Even though they were faint and from a distance, I still heard her. I saw in her movements on the court that she needed more from her conditioning classes. I heard in her stories of how she felt weak that she was at risk for injury. The basketball program at West Point averaged two to three ACL tears a season. What were they missing? Did they not hear the cries for help, or did they not understand how to interpret what they were being told? Love language has many forms. My jump stretch workouts kept me grounded through the last few years as I worked as a nurse, and they would help provide me not only with the drive to continue to work as a nurse but would also provide the fundamental information and knowledge needed to help my daughter and make a change in sports. I understood this was a huge number of ACL injuries, and this went on for years without anyone demanding change or even identifying this as a problem. When I was told this type of injury was a common occurrence by the medical team and by athletics, I explained that this should not be common. They agreed after they began to self-evaluate and wondered how they had gotten to that place where they accepted those numbers and how they could even speak to parents, telling them it was the norm. Someone needed the job to keep the women safe and to find the problem. Making administration aware that their program needed adjustment was necessary. Exposing certain trouble areas in the strength and conditioning program and revealing truths that the women were being overlooked in certain ways that was detrimental to their safety and health was critical. I had to respond. This is our opportunity in life, to help others in ways that sometimes seem beyond our qualifications. You may not even know you are qualified, but if you follow God's lead and respond when he calls you to respond, the qualification is there. Who was I to question and raise concern to a Division 1 women's basketball program? That was the response I got at first from people who did not want to be questioned, get involved, and admit truth. I knew who I was. I was built and called to respond to this. That was all that mattered to me. I had purpose in it. I recognized things and knew things that they could not imagine. I was not there to judge them. I was interested in change. I moved in faith and was bold about what I knew. This was who I grew into. It didn't happen overnight, but once I saw what needed done and that I needed to get involved, things happened. I was aggressive about showing up, meeting with people, and sharing what I knew could help the program. They wanted change once they were aware it was needed, which made the difference.

Those times in those rooms with those patients taught me so much about life. I had to believe the lessons had purpose and these patients had purpose, even though I didn't understand it all until years later. Changes to the basketball program were made, after all, and the young women were put in a better situation for growth. The amount of knee injuries did drop, and my Sabria did make a full recovery and was guided into proper training to have a very successful career in basketball following her injury. This is how God moves through time, place, person, and circumstance. Some people think these patients don't have purpose other than to lie in a bed, but during their forever sleep, God can channel love, build character, restore hope, teach confidence, and foster humility all at the same time, and this is the kind of power that moves between the patient and the nurse and extends out into the world.

Chapter 11

Prevention versus Pathogenesis

Lots had changed since the outbreak of COVID. Doctors would shudder when I got too close. Some were walking around in full body "space suits" complete with shields and face masks. Nurses were leaving their units on med-surg and coming to mine on mom and baby to try to escape any possibility of seeing the COVID infection, although it was found on my unit as well. They were coming prepared with excuses from their own doctor as to why they could not go into a COVID-positive patient's room. Whether it was because they were older, and therefore, susceptible, recovering from surgery, pregnant, or had an unhealthy immune system. We had a running list at the nurses' station of turns that the nurses took to go into COVID rooms. Every time you took care of a COVID patient, you put the date next to your name to make sure everyone took their turn. We were not heroes. This was why I decided to be on the COVID team. To not worry about taking "my turn" to go into a room or to worry about my health first before my patient's or to put my kid's health and safety over my neighbor's kids. Every single person was at risk. Some people had been diagnosed with things that put them at risk, but not all problems in people are diagnosed. We were all at risk. People just wanted to believe they had more of a right to stay away from the illness than someone else. This would be like saying that someone in a coma has no purpose in living, so why give them good care? We in America have a problem seeing anything other than what is directly in our faces, and this has caused a suppression. We don't want to search for answers or gain understating or a higher level of thinking. This was when I had volunteered to work down in the ICU and had COVID patients down there too in between my shifts on mom and baby. I did not worry about exposure. It was encouraged to take turns to not get overexposed. I saw this caused some problems because nurses started serving patients from the doorway or by using the phones to communicate to limit exposure. I cannot imagine all the patient neglect that came from this idea, but I did hear of some stories. There was a lack of faith in what God could do and that he was sovereign even during COVID pandemic.

There was a patient in the ICU who had an issue with bleeding. Her husband was not allowed to come see her because of the strict visiting hours during the pandemic and how the hospital wanted to regulate and limit people loving their families. God teaches us to love others with absolute purity, and this means there is no limit to how much we love somebody. Weak people violated this principle during COVID pandemic by putting restrictions on how people loved their families, and there is no justifying this course of action. I watched as they rushed this woman to a test and discussed the idea that she probably would not make it through the night. In the meantime, her husband had called the hospital and had already warned the front desk that he knew his wife was in trouble and he was coming to see her and did not care what the rules were. He wanted to see his wife one last time, and no one was going to stop him. The nurses talked, and the manager called the front desk letting them know to let the man in when he got there. They decided it was important for him to see her at that point, but why did he have to wait until then? It was so bad at that point. Why did he have to fight to see his wife of fifty years while she was on her deathbed? They were not honest with the man and did not give him appropriate updates because who knows a person's time of death besides God? The hospital chose to take the place of God during this time, and this is an unjustified and unwise decision. This man's own instincts and connection with his wife that comes from something more powerful than COVID proved to be his update on her condition. He knew she was close to death because they were one flesh. The hospital violated the bond of husband and wife and overlooked this profound spiritual connection. This realization was impactful, and it was shortly after seeing this craziness of people, taking ethical and moral obligations off the table to worship a virus, that I left the ICU. Like proteins can fold into their pathogenic forms, causing diseases and sickness, it was happening in the hospital as it turned into a place of business instead of a place that practiced health care. People had said to me that I was not only learning about the ICU, I was learning the ICU during COVID pandemic, and that was something completely different. Why was it different? That was how I came to understand that not only were the standards dropped during this time, but there was an awareness of the fact that standards were lowered, and everyone just folded into the change. They did not fight it. We allowed the decay of the health care system.

At some point it was said that 57 percent of the population had the COVID shot, and yet the COVID numbers were soaring. This had me thinking. I had heard about people, even people close to me, possibly getting sick or dying from getting the COVID shot, having seizures after, fainting out of the blue, having numbness and paralysis, heart attacks, strokes, cancer, PEs, and numerous other adverse effects. I decided to learn more about this vaccine and what it was about. My dad and I were very involved in my community and even across states to assist people with religious exemption so they could continue working without getting vaccinated. I even spoke up on the news and a local radio station about the unlawful mandates. My dad is a pastor, and so he and I worked as a team to counsel people during this time. We were the church to them. We used the Bible to help people to answer questions concerning how they believed and why they individually had their reasons for not choosing the COVID vaccination. I was able to get the word out about this through my website, christinahunter.com. This website was built by my friend who charged me nothing to do this, even though people charge upward of $10,000 to provide such a service. This website became a base for my work and a place where everything that I had been working on could be found because I knew there was more work for me to do.

The builder of my website's name is A.J., and he was still growing while I was growing. Since doing my website, learning all he could to get better, he has since built a website developing company called SWP, Skyline Web Productions. Through this time of helping me to promote my first book and my ministry of serving others through health and fitness of mind, body, and spirit, he had learned more and more about computers by being innovative, personalizing, building, and optimizing websites, engaging in the opportunity to help entrepreneurs start up and become successful in their business. A.J. was able to grow in the field of web design, web hosting, and website development by helping others achieve their goals. I see him as a team player and a genius. God has been building him for years, and I am so thankful for his willingness to stay in the building process. I call A.J. my angel, and he is one of the few true Americans left. He is God-fearing and aware of his talents but humble and respectful, fair, and trustworthy. He puts people over profit, and I could never repay him for how he encouraged me to keep going even when there seemed to be no hope in the fight. He can manage business accounts and works to make sure you are at the top of Search Engine Optimization. He gives IT assistance anytime it is needed for the people he services and is a good friend to me and my family, and this is the type of networking God provided for me as I stayed faithful. He will send you angels when you need them, so have faith.

People were so relieved for the wisdom, support, and faithfulness to God that was shown to them through the religious exemption program my dad and I provided during this time. This was how we loved the community. While so-called churches were masking up, closing their doors, and fueling the fear of COVID, we were going out into the public and speaking truth, bringing the church to people. People would text or send messages asking for help, and it differed based on their company of employment. I stayed flexible and reached out for information to be an asset even across several states. People were surprised at how much power they had. God says that we hold the power in our domain. We are not owned on this planet. We are free. This also means we are held accountable for our bodies, minds, and spirits, and how we treat others in these areas. People would text me at basketball games or practices or work, and I just got back to everyone because God provided that opportunity.

I kept information accessible and was able to guide people down the right path for their own personal situation. I let them know they had autonomy. They could learn the law and God's law so they could maneuver through, making the right decision for themselves. God allowed me to have a network of reliable information and people of courage that made this all possible. I believe this was the reason my dad had worked to earn his pastoral license years ago. It would be needed to qualify him as a reliable resource, even though God is who truly qualifies us to complete our mission. I also counseled people who got the shot because they believed they had to and wanted hope that they could be healthy again. There was hope for them, and they needed to know this. Once again, I learn these things even through people in a forever sleep. God is sovereign, and serving him means we hold power. The COVID shot, harmful or not, does not decide your future or give you barriers, whether taken or not. This may be hard to understand, but this is simple teaching, really. Yes, everything is relative, but God is the King even to relativity. I had people very close to me, even one of my best friends, who got the COVID shot. We loved each other through this time and helped each other stay hopeful. I would not recommend the shot or administer it and did not believe it to be beneficial or even a form of prevention after what I learned, but I also understand why people took it. It was very sad. The problem I saw was that it seemed to invite pathogenesis, not prevention of infection. I did expect and demand honest, informed consent when this shot came out, which I saw was not taking place. I did not support the mandating or administering of this mRNA and did not trust those who manufactured it. I had very close friends and loved ones who got the shot, and many had adverse effects from it. Many people I know got the shot even when they had a way out of it, and some were in positions where they really believed they were between a rock and a hard place. I prayed to God for my loved ones' protection after getting it, and I prayed for their healing and for the contents to remain powerless against them. I was concerned for their health and everyone's health in regards to COVID and the mRNA. I see everyone as family because I respect 1 Timothy 5:1. People were being overlooked for certain health screenings and surgeries because of the virus, and then the shot was believed to be causing sickness and disease too. All of this was concerning to me, and I chose to gain perspective. My concerns were not associated with the idea of aborted fetal cells being used in the manufacturing process (although this is disturbing). My attention was drawn to the biology and physiology related to the proteins and gene therapy used and the response from the body as a result of the mRNA being injected. I wanted to know what was going on with the shot and what it really was that I was being told to put in my body. My investigation included the pathophysiology of the proteins used and then the pathogenesis that could result. I did not trust a certain famous man, known for his development of computer software, and then his weaseling into making decisions in the medical field, earning the trust of people who believed he had medical knowledge and expertise. I believe he had neither. I watched him smirk in an interview, saying that the next outbreak would get more attention than the first. I wondered how anyone could trust him or the COVID shot he promoted when his history showed his goals were to make money and gain control even by way of false charity, talking about the pandemic before the pandemic even came about. This is the same man who had a desire to monopolize, gaining control in his areas of business, which other big businessmen and women took note of and tried to copy to also grow material wealth at the expense of others. This greed was growing, and I saw it personally as it made its way into the medical field, all the way to the bedside.

    I had read that a very prominent, influential, and popular leader in the church was encouraging everyone to get the shot because it was a "form of charity." He had previously been against it because of the idea that fetal cells were integrated into the manufacturing of the shot, but now it seemed he was claiming the fetal cell involvement was a form of taking one for the team, some kind of twisted form of sacrifice, saying we were all offering our bodies for the betterment of the whole. Since what he was saying had no biblical backing, I question why anyone would consider him a reliable spiritual source. This was yet another pandemic. So-called spiritual leaders were giving advice that did not come from God, bearing false witness. Churches were doing this all over, giving advice and teaching with no biblical backing, which is not Christianity, and yet they called it that. Many pastors canceled church and adopted the same policies as the world. It seemed viruses were spreading across our nation in different ways and taking many different avenues, but the core of the disease was all the same and stemmed from sin. It was said that the pharmaceutical company involved in manufacturing the shot believed in diversity, inclusion, and equity, but this is the opposite of what they promoted, saying that everyone needed to get the shot. They were telling people that these shots were used to cause your body to have an immune response, which would protect the body against disease. What about the perfect immune system that God created for us when we were born? A virologist talked about this and how we had all we needed at birth, so why the push for vaccines? Diseases came and ran their courses and then were gone, and this was how viruses worked throughout history. The vaccines were getting credit, instead, for the diseases dying off and our immunity doing what it was built to do. I saw the COVID shot as a way to advertise for something we didn't need but could make many companies lots of money. The lead organizations who promoted vaccines said they believed in people deserving to live healthy lives, and they wanted to provide affordable and effective means to do this, and this was used in reference to the mRNA. This is such a trickery and just a way to advertise for their business. It grew into extortion. My mom was kept from medical treatment for her decision to not take the COVID vaccine, and she was left by the medical field to die. God took her home, and I understand this was her time, but this does not excuse people for turning her away in a time of need. How was this promoting health?

  I began investigating the biology, physiology, and mechanics behind the key players inside the COVID shot. Everyone else seemed to be looking at the exact ingredients noted in the shots, calling them safe, but I wanted to understand the mechanism of action behind these shots and what was happening in the body in response to the genetic material. There were studies done at Texas University and John Hopkins that I looked into and included the National Library of Medicine as a resource for information obtained. The Human

Genome Database offered some important considerations as well. Using the knowledge I had from nursing and godly wisdom and counsel, I tried to understand more. I investigated what was studied and the information released, and I grew more and more curious as to why people trusted the shots, and yet I know they trusted people in their positions as so-called medical professionals. They wanted to believe people were looking out for them. The makers and pushers of the shot used this vulnerability along with the hope that people would not take the time and energy to investigate what was really going on. A wolf comes in sheep's clothing. It will sneak up on you and prey on your weakness, and this is what happened in our country. I understood that certain proteins were used in these shots, TDP-43 and FUS, which were the proteins used to deliver the vaccines into the body and cause the response of supposed immunity. These proteins were said to be associated with ALS and Alzheimer's disease as well as brain degeneration. When these coded messages were sent through the body when someone got jabbed with the COVID-19 shot, it was believed to be possible for these proteins to convert into their pathogenic forms, causing disease. If that was the case, wasn't it possible that these proteins could cause neurodegenerative diseases like ALS and Alzheimer's? It was found that these proteins could integrate into the human genes, potentiating the risk of a permanent change in a person's DNA, which then caused a change in genetic material. The genes become mutated, which could lead to a change in protein function within the person's body. It was thought to also manipulate the phenotypic characteristics of a person. Couldn't this then change their appearance, development, and behavior? Use your reasoning. Don't be afraid to think and come to a conclusion on things. I do trust science and the medical field is proven to not be an exact science. Some things we know to be true. Once again, relativity should be considered whenever studying science. I enjoy it and appreciate God's beautiful design. The one thing I have absolutely no doubt about is the fact that is loud and clear, and that is the fact that God's design is under attack. However, he will always be sovereign.

    A very respected and well-known doctor who claimed to be involved in the research of these COVID shots later called to advocate for the bioethics of giving it. He was once a supporter of the shots but later questioned the efficacy and safety of them and said it was more like gene therapy, and these jabs could be detrimental to people's health. He was shut down and received backlash for sharing his scientific expertise, but his convictions led him to continue to speak out about what he knew.

 Obesity was a bigger killer than COVID, so I was curious as to why this got more attention and why there was such a push for these shots, especially since they were experimental and served no good purpose. What's the catch? So far, as I learned there was no actual benefit to these shots but only had the potential to cause harm. I believe the makers of these shots depended on the distractions the American public were facing. While preoccupied with working hard, we were also being distracted by all the other pandemics including corruption of the church, school, big business, and sports. Would we be too tired to fight the pandemic in health care? In the body, once preoccupied by one virus, the immune system will be distracted fighting, and the body could then be infected by another virus that swoops in to cause even more harm. Was this understanding being used against the American people? During COVID pandemic, many people just went with the flow. Since this jab material was genetic and entered one's DNA, couldn't the changes that took place be passed onto generations, altering and disrupting familial heredity and traits and possibly causing diseases and disorders in future generations? A wide range of pathogenesis representing so many different types of diseases and disorders could develop, right away or later in life, as the proteins continued to replicate during the life cycle. This was a spiritual battle, waging war on God's human design. This was also happening in sports as people were thrusted into a devaluing system. People were involved in genetically modifying foods that were also shown to cause diseases, but making bigger and faster profit on food was the goal, and this has not been properly dealt with but, instead, allowed to continue. Some people were said to have been given a placebo shot. This way we did not see harmful effects to everyone all at once because this would have caused people who were already won over and trusting of the shot, to question the motives of the manufactures and pushers of it. More effort should have been put into curing people and treating them effectively while in the hospital, but this was not happening. Our focus was off.

After looking at different articles, podcasts, interviews, writings, and journals including *ALS News Today* and MedlinePlus, I began to better understand. I read many reports from doctors who had concern for what was happening in the body involving the ingredients in the shot. Our country had so many battles to face but seemed to be sitting on their sword. Draw your own conclusions. These are my understandings.

The protein FUS is a protein that regulates gene expression in the brain. I thought, *Couldn't the pathogenesis of these proteins result in brain disruption, degeneration, or even disruption of thought processes?* Studies were done to determine whether the two harmful proteins could embed themselves into a person's DNA as an mRNA is expected to do. It is said that the mRNA has specific sequences that may induce the turning of TDP-43 and FUS proteins into their pathogenic forms. Then they could embed themselves into a person's DNA and cause harmful diseases. Extreme protein deposits were reported to be found in people who died after getting the COVID shot. There are many mutations that have been found by these proteins in the past to cause sarcomas or cancerous tumors in people. If our country has done so much cancer research and has been successful in identifying the causative agents, why were we now injecting these agents into people's bodies by way of the COVID shot? Could it be so pharmaceutical companies and hospitals could make more money treating people for cancer? I knew that my mom was not given the treatment we knew she needed to heal but, instead, was forced to stay sick and keep coming back for more help and treatment as the doctors would charge her insurance each time, even though they denied her the very treatment that would provide her with a better quality of life. It was reported that many people developed aggressive cancers within months of getting the COVID shot and soon after died. The FUS protein is a gene that codes proteins, gives instructions to make protein, and is involved in making protein in the body. It attaches to DNA, and its job is to regulate transcription, which is the first thing to happen when genes make proteins. FUS also processes mRNA, oversees the types and versions of proteins made, and then transports them so they can further mature. It is also believed to be involved in several types of cancer in its pathogenic form. This made me understand why people were at risk of developing adverse effects from the shot that they were genetically predisposed to since this was genetic material entering the DNA and having had the opportunity to convert to pathogenic forms. This could explain why the adverse effects differ from one person to the next and why cancer could be found and at very advanced levels after the shot was administered because these proteins gave instruction to replicate. If they were able to disrupt the genetic system of a person also producing more proteins in the body, which were the building materials that keep us going, sustaining life, but also have the ability to fold into pathogenic forms of the proteins, could this not cause diseases if it replicates or puts out more pathogenic proteins? In other words, if blood clots ran in your family or you had cardiovascular familial history, could you be more likely to die from a PE, heart attack, or stroke after getting vaccinated? This vaccine formula using gene therapy was also thought to cause clotting and bleeding disorders as well as to induce autoimmune disease. If you have ALS in your family, were you more likely to develop neurologic-type diseases, as these proteins with pathogenesis possibility were multiplied through the transcription process? If you already had genetic kidney disease or renal failure in your family history, could your kidneys become diseased after getting the shot? The COVID-spiked proteins were hazardous and did cause many problems in and of themselves being compared to HIV, which causes AIDS, meaning it was destroying our immune system, allowing us to get sicker more often, not building up our immune system as they wanted us to believe. Why would you not look for ways to protect yourself from COVID or ways to kill the virus (which were available) if it got inside of you, instead of actively and voluntarily putting it in your body along with genetic material capable of alternating your DNA and causing your body to replicate diseased proteins inside of you? I now understood why I was just inwardly opposed to putting this thing in my body, and the more boosters, the more likely you were to have problems arising, putting more of these proteins and genetic material in your body, continuing to manipulate the DNA God designed specifically for you. Viruses were getting worse and worse, seemingly stronger in nature, which was predicted through this plan. People seemed to be sicker than ever, always suffering from a cold or stomach bug or bowel issue. This was bound to happen after the shedding and how viruses need to learn to adapt to survive, but people were made to believe it was something else to fear instead of a direct effect of sin in our country. We were making ourselves sicker. The more vaccines that went out, the more shedding, the more disease. I heard about a doctor who ran a clinic to heal people. He talked about how vitality had dropped in people because of the COVID jab itself and from the shedding of the virus and that both did damage. He claimed the methods he used restored vitality and could help detox the body. He explained the virus, contaminants, and other intruders turned genes on and off, disrupting our whole system. He explained that no one should live with diabetes and that it is easy to cure by removing the attackers in the body, responsible for turning on and off these switches in the genes, restoring normal and appropriate function in the body. Why does the medical field tell us otherwise? Why do they teach that diseases such as autoimmune disorders have no cure and that diseases like diabetes cannot be cured or maybe that the root of the problems cannot be traced? Could it be because diabetes, especially type 1, which is on the rise after COVID and the shots, keeps people slaves to the medical field and makes this organization an extreme amount of money along with manufactures of insulin pumps and all the equipment and technology involved in that, and the pharmaceutical companies that sell the insulin and meds needed to sustain these people's lives? Why not pay the a few hundred bucks to this doctor to run a genetic scan and tell what can be done to possibly be cured of chronic and seemingly incurable diseases? Why are people not looking into these methods and options? Why are people staying sick? We degrade our bodies sometimes without even realizing it, but God teaches us to be careful of this (1 Corinthians 6:19–20). It is our duty and even a command to honor God with our bodies. Wouldn't this include finding out how we can do better for ourselves and our health? These are my thoughts and why I opposed it. I encourage you to answer the questions in this book for yourself. I am sharing my perspective. I believe COVID and the shot were attacks on mankind, and the control that people allowed the devil to have was disturbing, but I continue to have hope for change, and God is still supreme. People who got the COVID shot should know they can be healthy again. Our country can be healed. God is the ultimate healer, so if you have a concern for yourself or have health problems that you believe may be due to this shot or the virus, pray for healing. I have been answered when I asked God to heal me when I needed it. Some people got the shot, and this was something they believed they had to do for whatever reason. I understand. Some people were in situations where they truly believed they had no other choice, and if they were to stay on God's path, they had to get the shot. This was where some people found themselves. Others believed it was right to get the shot. I know people in all these situations. None of us are above lapse of judgment or out of reach of answered prayer, so I say let's pray for each other. There is so much power in that!

Chapter 12

Being Different

I never paid too much attention to getting sick. People who know me know I will work through almost anything. I never have an excuse to stop or slow down. In fact, I remember not wanting to take off from work when getting my thyroid gland removed. I was pregnant at the time. A cyst on my thyroid was discovered, and the doctor thought it was too risky for the baby for me to have the surgery. I had to wait until I delivered, which was about seven months later. By the time I could have surgery, the cyst was the size of an egg or a small lemon and took over the whole right side of the gland in my neck. The whole gland on the right side had to be removed. Apparently, my vocal cord nerve was very small, and they did try to protect and preserve it during my surgery, but it was not easy, and the cyst had begun to push the esophagus and trachea off to the left, which did cause some discomfort and trouble that I overlooked during the pregnancy to get my son to term. It was important to get the cyst out before permanent damage was done. It was becoming dangerous. The size of the cyst caused changes to the anatomy in my neck, and swallowing was difficult.

After surgery, I lost my voice for about a month. I was about eight weeks postpartum and ten days post–thyroid surgery when I went back to work. I was still breastfeeding and still had my neck lined with stitches and could only whisper, but I went back to work anyway. I could not afford to stay off any longer. When I went back to the surgeon for my follow-up, he said, "You didn't go back to work yet, did you?" This was a rhetorical question because he knew how I was. I said, "Yes, I did." He just shook his head at me and rolled his eyes. I did not need a return-to-work slip because my employer didn't even know I had the surgery. They knew I had the baby. I figured my leave of absence was a two for one. They saw my stitches and heard my whisper of a voice, but I could not explain much at the time anyway, so they did not ask. My coworkers knew some of the story. This was how I was. It was so tiring to strain my voice to talk to the patients, and my neck muscles were exhausted by the end of the day, but I did it. This task was much easier than my life at home and what I just went through to have that surgery and the recovery after just having my fifth baby, so I was built to push through.

The building process God had done in me was obvious. I struggled in life at times, but I trusted that God had a plan. So let me back track to explain. The morning of my thyroid surgery, I arranged to get a ride to the hospital from my mom and my aunt. They stayed with me while I got prepped and then saw me off to surgery. They thought it was strange that Bobby did not want to be there with me to see me off to surgery, but I just said he had to work because that is what he told me. This was back during the time that he still did not seem to understand his role as my husband, and these are the times I was so eager to keep fighting to show him his worth and mine too. He saw me as an investment, I think. Maybe a piece of property that he owned. I had to be tough so I could show him I was someone different. I had to train tough to be tough, and I knew all my efforts would pay off. I was so unsettled to leave the five kids, especially my new baby, and was afraid I'd never come home, which I think was just the lack of sleep and postpartum hormones talking, but I just put one foot in front of the other and trusted God to see me through. I needed my husband Bobby there with me, but I also knew he would not be supportive anyway. He never liked when I was sick or unable to function at my best. So I just chose to find grit and keep going, one foot in front of the other to the operating room after hugs and well-wishes from those two supportive women in my life. I was so thankful to my mom and aunt that day for their support, and this I will cherish forever. My dad was able to watch my kids that day, so I had that to be thankful for too.

    Once I got taken back. The nurse told me to take all my clothes off. I whispered to her that I had just had a baby and had a pad on, and she understood. She just looked at me and whispered back, "Oh, okay, honey that's fine." I was so vulnerable. I felt so small as the patient and in that condition, with my body tore up and tired. I was so glad to have a nice nurse. I can see women and have a heart for them because of what I've been through, and this was, again, God building me to be able to have humility and gratitude and to know what it feels like to need others to be gentle and loving toward me. Learning all of this allowed me to extend love to other women and to be understanding and sensitive to their needs. I had to stay for one night after my thyroid surgery so they could watch my bleeding and swelling to make sure my airway was protected. Bobby came to visit me for an hour that evening, and I was so glad to see him, but when he got there, he put on the basketball game and sat in front of the TV in front of my bed while I sat in the bed with drains hanging and an incision across my neck. He left shortly after arriving. I called him the next day for a ride home, but he said he was at work and could not come get me and to find my own way home. I already had my discharge papers and was embarrassed that I did not have a ride home. I knew how this looked from a nursing standpoint, and I tried to act quick so they didn't know I was stuck there. I didn't want to ask family or friends because I just wanted my husband. They had helped me so much already. Honestly, looking back, these were the hardest times of my life and a time I felt very alone. Everything was hard. I trusted God for everything, for every move and every decision, and my affliction is what built my relationship with God and why I am so close to him. My dad was there at my house that day to watch my kids again, thankfully, and he was always there for me just like an earthly angel, a physical representation of God. I sat at the edge of the hospital bed and felt desperate. I called my brother Dom, and I whispered through the phone that I needed a ride. I had no voice but wasn't used to that yet. He said, "What?" He couldn't hear me talking. He finally caught on and was glad to come to pick me up. He has a presence about him, and when he blasted into my hospital room, like, "Hey, Tina, I'm here," it was like coming home, even though we hadn't left yet. My brother Dom is a good caregiver to anyone who needs help. He drove me to the pharmacy, and I walked in to get my pain medicine because I knew my husband wouldn't do this for me, and whenever I asked for help, he got angry, and this only made things harder. My neck was so stiff, swollen, and bruised. I looked like a dazed Frankenstein with bruising and stitches going across my neck, a whisper for a voice. I carefully walked into the pharmacy, which was in the same hospital I worked in. I was under strong narcotics, and as I sat in the chair, waiting for my meds, aware of how hard my recovery would be and all that was waiting for me at home and in life, I just realized that was my life, and I just did what I had to do. My parents and my siblings were my sense of security, and my kids were my hope. My circle was small and I was blessed.

At home, I was not supposed to be lifting because it could cause more bleeding in my throat and neck, especially with all the manipulation that was done in surgery, but I had a new baby and was breastfeeding, plus I had four other kids, so this really was impossible, and I was not sure how I would keep up with my postsurgery restrictions, but I did try to be careful so I could continue to be a good mom and wife. I had to sleep in a recliner for a couple weeks because to lie down was unbearable. One time, during my recovery, I remember waiting too long to take my pain medicine. I did not get much sleep with my new baby and breastfeeding, so when I finally fell asleep for a nap, I must have just slept through the time for my next dose of pain medicine. By the time I woke, I literally could not get off the chair because the pain was so intense and I was so tired. My head and neck felt like they weighed a hundred pounds. I felt trapped in that chair. I panicked. I asked Bobby, who was close by in the other room, to please get to the cabinet to get my medicine, but he yelled at me and said I needed to take care of myself because he had things to do. He did not want me to be dependent on him. He was used to me being strong and doing everything, and this was who I still needed to be. Bobby did not love me back then. This was how I could relate to so many women who did not have the support of a man after having a baby, and I wanted to show them God's love in me toward them and wanted them to have hope because that was what got me through all those times when my husband struggled to know his role. This was how love transferred from the bedside. Bobby is different now and still has his "down" times when that old man creeps in, but I remind him he is past that. He was young back then when I had thyroid surgery, twenty-eight maybe, although maturity does not always follow chronological age. He was selfish, and he did not know God the way I did, but I had faith that he would one day love me the way God did. So I managed to muster up the strength and got out of that chair and made it to the kitchen and got to the prescription and took the pain pills.

This was why going back to work was not that hard. No one knew what I went through at home. Work was just another thing on my plate, but it was all hard. Taking care of others made me feel better and helped me not to dwell on my stressors at home or my own ailments. Plus I had bills to pay, so I told myself I just had to do it. I bonded with moms and wanted to ease some of their burden while they were on my watch in the hospital. It was therapy for me to take care of others the way I wanted to be cared for. Seeing the other nurses push through the day was encouraging too. After about six weeks, my voice was back. Raspy for a while and I could not yell, but talking was getting easier. My neck muscles would be sore at the end of the day, but they got stronger over time. I was thankful to have a voice at all because I was told I may never get it back. I did not know at the time if Bobby would ever change. I only had hope he would, and this was how I grew in faith because I kept going, believing things would get better. I knew that I had no excuse to give up, and with God all things were possible. Whether I had Bobby on my side or not did not change who I was. I had to love God first, then myself, Bobby, and others; and this meant doing my best every day. Having Quintin really taught me I was capable of love on another level with all I went through, and he was the sweetest baby. Loving him was so rewarding, and that love was reciprocated by him, giving me a reason to keep fighting and giving my best.

This is how I was raised to be, not to make a big fuss about myself or my needs but to keep going. Today we are taught to stay home if we do not feel good. We are taught to baby ourselves and that being strong and committed to discipline is a danger to other people. It is not true. God taught me that to be a good team player at home and at work, I need to have more confidence and push through on the hard days, not so I can have more for myself like shopping days, vacations, or popularity, but so that I can make the lives around me better and they can know the truth too. I learned a lot about my husband during this time. To be honest, I love that man more than life itself, and I never saw him as he was in those dark times. I saw him as God did, and I knew he needed to change, and my hope was always that he would. How would he change if he did not see the difference in me? How would he know there was another way to live if he did not see this displayed in me, the closest person to him? Everyone left him when they did not like who he was. No one seemed loyal to him. I had to be that for him. I made mistakes too, and that is what I had to remember. I was not perfect. My husband began to see me, and he even began to call me "different" on a regular basis. It took many years and much heartache for him to appreciate this about me because he did not want to change or believe that there was more to do in life than to just get by. He did not have much support growing up and got used to settling for less, but now he wanted more for himself and began to trust me. We all have hurt on some level in our relationships and in life, but by always taking for ourselves and this being our goal in life, to be comfortable, to have constant pleasure, we are taking away from others. I knew that Bobby had been hurt in his life and wanted so bad to believe that he had worth, and I was determined to let him see that, no matter how long it took. I had to make sacrifices. I had to toe the line. He was someone I could invest in. He was valuable; he needed to believe it for himself.

We do not have good support for the development of men of good character in our country. It is a dying culture to be a man of good character. It seems that most men have lost focus on what is important and, instead, look to make lots of money and have what they believe is a successful business, a big title, and lots of time to relax and enjoy whatever gives them pleasure. They do not strive to have that higher level of life and fellowship where God holds the standard and where true power and control are available in him, but we can experience this in ways that are a benefit to us and others. These are the people I pray to meet, the people who are different and whom I can network with to show others there is a better life out there. Society raised my husband. Yes, he always had the choice to change, but he became what he was taught to be, self-centered, looking out for himself and on guard to protect himself from people out to get him. He was made to believe he was a victim of circumstance, and he craved comfort. He needed it constantly. So I always told him he lived in "Bobby's world." I invited him to come out of that world and to see what else God had for him. He grew up starving for attention, and I grew up with lots of attention. His parents split when he was young, and his dad never stayed in contact. This may even be worse than not knowing your dad at all. To have a dad who you knew and who you loved as a small child and then is suddenly gone is effective in the destruction of one's idea of self-worth. Bobby did understand that part of this disconnect came from his parents' decision to divorce, and his mother moving several states away from his dad made contact difficult. It was not impossible to keep in contact, but the truth was it would have been hard to remain connected, and his dad just did not try hard enough to see him. Bobby ended up trying to take for himself as he got older. He worked to satisfy a craving. He wanted to be worthy. He wanted to be enough to be loved and cared for. He wanted to be worth someone trying hard. I wanted to let Bobby see that his craving could be satisfied in knowing he would never be enough because none of us are. This is what grace is for. He started to understand.

I longed to give back to people because so many people gave for me as I grew up, especially my parents. They taught me to pay for my own college tuition but to go through an accelerated program, so I worked harder but paid less and got done quicker. This taught me that what I needed I had within me. I learned perseverance. Even as I got older, society tried to teach me in ways that were not beneficial to my growth. Many nurses believed that they had to get their bachelor's degree because that is what many hospitals made them believe. I believed what my parents told me, and that was to follow God and not to believe everything society was selling. I was offered many jobs as a nurse even after 2020 when facilities were pushing bachelor's degrees. I have a two-year degree, and I would not go back to school spending thousands of dollars to just continue doing what I already do. I had years of experience in the field and taking an English class and some math would not qualify me as a better nurse. Everyone knows that, but for some reason, we play into the world's game. It was not more knowledge gained; it was just advertisement pushed hard by making people believe they needed what was offered. The hospital could brag about how many nurses had continued their education, which was not needed to be a great nurse, and the colleges could rake in money from nurses who believed they needed the title to keep working. Some hospitals made nurses sign a contract, committing to getting their bachelor's degree within two years of hire, but not all hospitals did this. Ones whose value was in status and not in family, hard work, and people, did this. The problem, I would see later, would be in those who had knowledge but were forever learning without acknowledging truth; therefore, their learning was useless. This is what our country pushes, useless knowledge and forever learning without it manifesting into anything truly productive. This way, the top leaders believe they can make all the money and keep all the control. It isn't true that more college builds better people, but it does cause a lot of distress for our country, and the lies keep people bound by their desire to keep climbing that ladder that will never lead to anywhere good.

My husband is always growing, and he is someone I am impressed with and thankful for. He worked his way up to the job he has now by paying attention and applying his knowledge over the years, building a resume of hard work and years of service in factory work and industrial maintenance. He now has a good job in a chemical plant. He trusted God, and doors opened to gain education. He just kept an open mind over the years, believing against what he thought he was, worthless. He didn't have a lot of faith, but he had a little, and that was enough. He asks me why I picked him, "a dirty, smelly boy from the ghetto." I tell him I never saw him that way, and he always smelled good to me. I saw him and where he lived and knew him as my "diamond in the rough." He was told when he was young to act like he had learning disabilities, and he would get more from society for free. This was how he thought he could help his family. He didn't even learn to read until the tenth grade, always getting pushed through and not invested in, since he didn't try hard or show any interest. People didn't know or care what his upbringing was like. Bobby just had to see things different than how he believed things were. He was more amazing than he knew. He was not a product of his environment. He was smart, caring, hardworking, and could survive under harsh conditions. He was an overcomer. He was the opposite of a cuttlefish but many times found himself acting like one. He always found ways to give into desires, still holding onto some beliefs from his childhood, which are lies. He didn't always treat me right. Now that we are older and he is finally gaining perspective, and acknowledging truth, I can talk to him, and he shares good insight, and we can finally grow and learn together. I am not against learning or gaining more college degrees. I am against forcing people to do this, and only on certain terms when no one is enriching the person earning the degree but passing them through a program to make profit for themselves. Bobby gave me many reasons to leave, but I didn't want to give up on him. This is marriage, and he still calls me "different."

Chapter 13

The Day My Mom Saved My Life

COVID was looked at as a phenomenon, and although there were details concerning COVID that made it stand out, I often wondered why the nursing field looked differently at it than other challenging and lethal diseases. I had taken care of patients for years with bad infections and who were in isolation. Nurses have been putting on the isolation garb to go into rooms for years. But we never wore these getups in the hallways and out and about, and we certainly did not reuse this equipment after going into these rooms. There have been outbreaks even in Bible times, and the reason for the outbreak was always the same, sin. It was no different with COVID. Being fearful with all the gowns and masks offers a reminder of death and disease to our minds as we are doing normal everyday activities like grocery shopping, exercising, working, and driving our cars. This was a gimmick, an advertisement, a way to force panic so people wouldn't think or use good reasoning. We as humans will always be exposed to things that can kill us; we need to correspond with God and walk in faith when we encounter these events.

People would ask me if I was afraid of COVID and could not understand how I could answer "no." The unveiling of the understanding that I was different from others and the searching for more knowledge and understanding as to why I believed the way I did led me to look back at a time when I had gotten very ill. It all began one day in the springtime of 2005, on a particular day while I was still working on the critical care unit. I started to feel like I was getting sick one day while home with my family. Nothing more than a cold or upper respiratory tract infection, I thought. I continued as normal until my condition worsened. Finally, I decided one afternoon that I needed to take a break. I took some Tylenol, and then I told my husband, Bobby, I had to lie down. He took my two kids at the time, Sabria, four and Dylan, six months, to the backyard to play on the swing set while I got a nap. Those were still the days he got annoyed if I was sick, so I needed to get better fast. I woke up from my short nap, and I felt weird. My whole body felt off-track. My heart was racing and beating through my chest. I felt feverish and took my temperature, and it was 103. I knew the Tylenol should still be in my system and should be working by now, so this was very concerning to me. I tried to call for my husband, Bobby, from the bed, but I was too weak to yell. This alarmed me. I could not get out of the bed. I was so weak. My body just would not move. To walk the distance from my bedroom to the bathroom across the hall to call for my husband from the window was an impossible task. I was stuck in my bed, unable to move. I knew this was bad. I had the house phone next to my bed, and apparently, Bobby did not have his cell phone on him because I tried to call him, but I got no answer. I called my mom as I had a feeling of impending doom, like I was going to die. I just remember telling her what my temperature was and that I had already taken Tylenol. I said I was afraid that something was wrong. She did not let the conversation go any longer and said, "I will be right there."

There were only a few phone calls I made to my mom over the years that stick out in my mind. This was one of them. Another one I made was when I was in labor with Dylan and yet another one when I was in labor with Sophia, my third child. These were times I thought I might be in labor but was not sure if it was time to go to the hospital yet. My mom knew by my voice and said, "It is time. Go to the hospital." She was right, and she exercised storge on my behalf. So when she showed up to my house, Bobby was shocked to meet her outside because he did not know what was going on and that I was so sick. This was during the time that Bobby and my mom did not get along. She did not believe he took good care of me. He did not appreciate her criticism. They tolerated each other for my sake. My mom had brought my brother Mike along, and Bobby and Mike got me under my armpits and assisted me to the car. I could not bear weight on my own and could not hold my body up. I was so weak. This illness came on hard and so fast that I could not believe it, but I knew without help, I would die.

    Mike and Bobby rushed me to the closest ER, and they immediately took me back to a room. When they hooked me up to the monitor, it read that my heart rate was 180 beats per minute at rest, and my oxygen level was in the low nineties. I knew this was bad and knew my heart rate was in a dangerous range, about triple what it normally was, and in my nurse's mind I thought, *Oh man! I need a Cardizem drip!* Sure enough, I heard from behind the curtain the doctor telling my nurse to get a Cardizem drip ready, and this was when reality was setting in that I would be admitted, probably to my own unit that I worked on! I knew that I must have had an infection that found its way to my bloodstream, and this caused it to go wild and just pollute my entire body. I knew I was septic. They decided first to try a fluid bolus to see if they could get my heart rate down with hydration, and this did bring it down a little. I was still tachycardic but did not need the drip at that point. Then they decided I was stable enough to transfer me by intensive mobile to the main hospital downtown, where I worked. My body could go into septic shock, and I knew I only had a small window of opportunity to get help before my organs shut down, and my limbs would be lost, then eventually, I would die. Thankfully, the hospital got infectious disease, cardiology, and pulmonology on my case fast, and those doctors along with my family doctor were able to figure out what biological intruder had attacked me and treated my infection with IV antibiotics and a beta blocker for my heart. I was only twenty-three years old, so I think my age and overall good health did help me battle this illness, but I also know God woke me up from that nap that day and gave my mom the intuition to know I needed help.

    I had to stay in the hospital for a few days on a monitored sister unit to mine and then went home and was readmitted once more because my body was just not ready to go home yet the first time.

This infection threw me for a loop, and I was just not improving very quickly. I was breastfeeding at the time so that sprinkled difficulty into the situation. I did not have my pump with me while I was in the hospital and was too weak to pump anyway. I woke up in the hospital room with my gown drenched in my own breast milk, and I was not permitted to shower because I was on a heart monitor. My breasts were engorged and swollen, and Bobby brought my pump in from home, and I was able to pump and dump to get relief. I never owned one of those fancy electric breast pumps. I only had a manual pump for all six kids, and I was thankful for it.

I had to stay on heart medicine for a while and eventually made a full recovery. Just like when your spiritual heart gets hurt and it must recover from trauma and must believe it can be healthy again, your physical heart will sometimes keep beating fast or in an unhealthy rhythm until it realizes the threat is gone and it can beat normally again. The medicine trains the heart that it can relax and beat normally again. Sometimes we must train our spiritual hearts after trauma. Bobby needed to do this in his own life so he could love me and the family alongside my mom. We need to know that the threat of trauma is gone and we can love ourselves and others without putting up a wall, limiting our efforts. It was interesting, even to the doctors, that even though I dressed according to the rules, with all the garb of masks, gowns, and gloves and followed the protocols when entering my isolation patient's rooms, that did not stop a droplet from finding its way into my body. They were intrigued that I managed to get so sick, and it was a good reminder that we are human beings and we are at risk of getting sick, and it is possible to be on death's door even when we are protected by all the protection and protocols this world offers. God is our protector and healer.

This is why I was not afraid of COVID. You can do everything seemingly right and still get sick. You can think you covered all bases but really did not. You can have knowledge, be healthy and young, and still get sick. You do not need to fear death. When it is time for us to die, we will. If my mom had been afraid to be around me because I had a fever and could be contagious, I might have died that day. My mom was not a perfect mom, but she did not have to be.

She just needed to move when God said to move, and she accomplished things, even helped to preserve my life. I believe she saved my life that day because she heard the concern in my voice and she moved in faith to be by my side. She did not wear a mask to come see me or wear gloves when she touched me. Her example has taught me much about being a good mom, nurse, and woman. Although moms fail every day, including myself, God gives us enough grace to continue having opportunities to make a difference in our kids' lives, and this is what we need to cling to, and this is what we need to influence on others. It was not my time to leave earth. God decided to heal me and supply people around me to act with intuition and love; otherwise, I have no doubt I would have died right there in my bed while my kids and husband played outside. My heart would have eventually given out, and I would have gone into cardiac arrest. That was not the plan for me. I did not take much time off from work and went back to that same unit and worked for another three years there. I did not wear masks at home or in the hallways, afraid of getting sick again. I went back to the same place where it was suspected I got the illness from, and I kept working. This was who I was because God taught me to have faith in him. Things happen for a reason, and there is always a reason to be hopeful and thankful but never a reason to be afraid. Be careful and protect yourself but don't live in fear. Be ready to die, so when you do, you and God are not meeting for the first time. COVID was not a word I knew until a good fifteen years after this experience. But I knew I had gotten sick for a reason, even back then. I just did not know why at the time. I trusted that God had a reason, and it was to teach me not to be afraid of being sick or dying because when it is time, he will take me home, and that is all that matters. That is everything. I even remember getting visitors at the hospital while I was sick with that bad infection. It was my childhood friend Jason's parents, Monica and Donnie. Monica was the woman I talked about in my first book, my mom's best friend since the age of five, who told me the story about how God took the snow so she could drive through a blizzard to see her mom in the hospital one time. Her story inspired my prayer to God when I was on that freeway in the mountains, alone, in a whiteout, coming home from

West Point, New York, after visiting my daughter Sabria. I asked God to "please take the snow." He did take the snow. It just disappeared, and I made it home safe. Monica shares the same faith I do, and that is why she visited me in the hospital, and that is why I will always remember that love is more powerful than any sickness or disease and stronger than any storm.

Chapter 14

The Beginning of the Letters

COVID was not the only disease that was experienced at the hospital; the disease of corporate compliance is thriving. The system that has been designed to control health care is a broken system. It relies on checklists and protocols that force us all into becoming robots, and the more we come away from reasoning, the more vulnerable we become to the prince of the air. I had grown over the years as God was preparing me for what I would find myself doing. In 2022 I wrote letters and sent them all the way up the chain, asking for improvements to be made on the unit I worked on in the hospital. After meetings were had and the important facts we brought up were not validated and taken care of promptly and efficiently, I pushed the letters up the chain. My friend and I talked about how the attitudes of those in leadership had changed toward us after we brought up serious safety issues going on, and that started the retaliation and suppression I received for speaking truth. We both confronted the toxic work environments we were working in, and this brought on a sense of discord between us and those in charge. There is supposed to be protection for nurses that speak up, but this is a false sense of security, and I knew what I was getting into. She knew years ago she could not work there as she furthered her license in nursing to an advanced practice nurse, knowing they did not value her principles and work ethic. She grew out of that place, and once that happens to you, you must move on so that you are not held back. This means you have taken new shape, and you no longer fit in a position you were once in. She ended up working hard and finishing school and then opening her own business to serve the community on her terms, with dignity and honor. I, on the other hand, stayed where I was but was engulfed in my mission to make change or at least make waves, believing I would be used by God even if it did not seem easy or possible. I had to believe in the building process he had me on. I was hoping to grow up enough in faith to leave and to make bigger change and take on new missions. It was my calling. Whether it would manifest change in those around me at the time, I did not know, but I kept being honest, working hard, learning every day, and walking in faith. I wanted to show people the power of exposing truth and being committed to persevere to see results even when you are attacked. With God, no one can really hurt you. Even though I had begun this journey five months earlier in August with my first meeting, and now it was January, still some changes had been made, but more importantly, people's eyes were open to the value of picking a side and staying on it, confident that good will triumph over evil in the end, and I want to represent the good side no matter how successful the easy side seems at the time. This shows true integrity by maintaining your faith and staying grounded through adversity. I saw many people's true colors through this time. My boss got caught in the middle and seemed to be trying to impress leadership even though they were not being honest. Open lines of communication are only had by those who are confident in their decision-making. If they know there are discrepancies between who they are and who they say they are, they will not communicate honestly. This snowball effect of poor leadership started at the top of the hill and rolled down, collecting sticks and rocks and all kinds of debris along the way from all the other leaders at the top of the hill down to the bottom. People in these positions were not willing to do what it took to run a safe and people-centered facility. My boss was at the bottom of the hill and caught the brunt of that snowball. They wanted to blame someone for problems the faulty system created. If they admitted their system was faulty, they would have to change, and they were too comfortable for that. Their comfort would prove to cause the discomfort of many others, and it is like the pathogenic protein that replicates and causes disease in a person's body. Just like COVID and the shot are biological tools the devil uses against humanity, corporate compliance that destroys workers, patients, and families is also waging war on America. Take heart. Make change. Start standing up for what is right because you will always be protected by God when doing this. In the end, he always wins.

Here is a close example of the letters I wrote to leadership hoping for change.

Letter number 1:

> I would like to address some very important issues with you concerning the current condition of the mom and baby unit at the hospital I currently work at as a registered nurse. Many doctors and seasoned nurses have left our facility to escape dysfunction, and those who remain continue to talk about mistakes that are being made repeatedly and how these mistakes are not taken seriously and no plans are being made for improvement, causing the problem of mental and physical exhaustion of nurses and lack of quality of care to patients. Many hospitals, at least five of them in the surrounding area, have closed their OB departments over the last few years. Since our OB department moved several years ago to another location, many things have changed, and we are serving a much larger area. We are constantly overflowing with patients, which has our nurses split between several units at times and overwhelmed with patient care assignments. The OB department is very unorganized and chaotic. We have been waiting for improvements and plans to be made to construct a more suitable arrangement for these patients and for the nurses, but nothing has changed over the years. Our nurses are in distress. I must reach out for help and support as I am moved and inspired by a specific Bible verse.

James 4:17 says, "Anyone, then, who knows the good he ought to do and doesn't do it, sins."

My conscience has led me to search for truth concerning the working conditions on the mom and baby unit at my hospital. Being a nurse at this facility for eighteen years and on the mom and baby unit, specifically, for fourteen years, I know it is my responsibility, as God calls me to a higher standard, to respond to the immoral treatment of the staff on my unit and how the quality of care has deteriorated over time. The lack of response that our unit has received from leadership over several years has created a dangerous environment and has allowed the fostering and development of a deep-seated culture, which does not support quality patient care and which does not ensure nurses' good health and well-being. As I tell of what I have encountered and learned through my searching for answers, try to gain perspective and understand that if you are reading this or listening as I speak, you may now be accountable to God for what you are being made aware of. This revelation brings opportunity to choose to make a change for those who are involved.

AWHONN has developed methods to plan, lead, and implement a positive and flexible staffing matrix. After staffing issues were identified, studies were conducted to uncover and expose the problems with burned-out nurses and poor quality of care to patients across America. Nurses and patients were heard through these studies, and changes were needed. Not only were guidelines developed and then revised but were then made into the standard.

A whole panel of nursing experts from AWHONN have reportedly responded to the negativity in nursing in our country and have offered support through the drawn-up standard. It is imperative that those who were called into leadership at our hospital acknowledge truth and respond to the poor conditions on our unit. True leaders are led by conviction of conscience. There are very specific characteristics that set apart a true authentic leader from an impostor. A true leader who embraces reality and confronts problems is different from one who talks of themselves as if they display these attributes but truly does not engage in them on a regular basis at home or at work. With careful consideration and listening to staff, the necessary changes to our unit can and should be put in place, reflecting authentic leadership. I am thankful for the standards that were drawn up and the grids and blueprints that were made to support true leaders in developing a safe and healthy work environment to serve nurses and patients. Why have they not been implemented on my unit? I am on a mission to bring change and to also question the evaluation processes of the very popular accrediting organizations who have given our hospital undue credit and the state services that are required to authorize continued practice of safe health care facilities. It is my understanding that the goal is to promote the gold standard of quality health care and a positive and health-conscious environment for nurses to thrive in. I do believe some very specific details may have been overlooked when our unit was evaluated for and given accreditation from these organizations. How did we meet criteria when no plans were made to change what is going on? Nurses are not satisfied or given an environment to thrive in, and the patients do not receive quality care, as best practice is not supported.

Here are some very specific attributes and characteristics of a true, authentic leader: inspiring; able to engage; a developer; ethical and civic-minded; effective communicator; loyal; courageous; has integrity, empathy, honor, passion, integrity, authenticity, creativity, influence, transparency, and intelligence; is a delegator, humble, confident, accountable, and a good decision-maker; is flexible, resilient, goal-oriented, and always learning; hopeful; faithful; full of gratitude; dependable; self-aware; a self-reflector; responsible; decisive and honest; and trustworthy.

I have heard it said that management is about persuading or causing people to do things they do not want to do; however, true leaders inspire people to do things that were believed to be impossible. For some reason, micromanaging is worshipped in health care, and this lowers the quality of care.

It takes courage to engage in authentic leadership that results in merited boldness, and this is what our unit needs. Boldness presents itself as a result of the overflow of leadership and inspirational qualities in a person. It is a state of being. If a person does not practice to strengthen leadership traits, they will not build in the person, and true boldness never develops. When someone refuses to do the work of a leader but wants to be recognized as one, they try to mimic what a leader is, and this can be easily recognized as you watch their actions and see how they display unmerited boldness. They will try to look confident and sound convincing but do not put solid foundational values into practice. There ends up being nothing to stand on because they do not choose the harder right over the easier wrong as an everyday practice. This encourages development of an unstable environment, and if attention is not paid to changing mindset, behavior, and most importantly heart, what was built will eventually crumble. This is what is happening on my unit. It has been reported to me by my peers that leadership has discouraged them from writing safe cares, which identify and reveal mistakes and safety issues on the unit. When a safe care was written concerning the neglect of a patient by a doctor in the OR, the nurse was told that we should not write a safe care on a doctor, supporting even worshipping pretentious, self-righteous attitudes. We should value our knowledge and education that we have gotten over the years by practicing good works. If we have been only pretending to mature, we should not be soliciting to the public that we are an advanced, safe, and dependable facility. We have much to learn about being humble, authentic leaders in the community, and God is our witness in this.

It is time for self-reflection when our leadership can come to work and have a huddle first thing in the morning, telling us to work quickly and efficiently to move out discharges so we can move the overflow patients into rooms on our unit, while our assignments, at times, could easily be cut in half according to AWHONN standards. Having leadership smile at us and say we are doing a good job while we are continuously having a workload, full of unrealistic expectations, is not honorable. Telling us that they hate the matrix we are using yet implementing it every day is not being trustworthy of a leader. We were told last week, September 8, 2022, that our patient satisfaction scores are low. Of course, we were told that since we had around 346 deliveries last month, it is understood that we were busy, but the response from our patients is unacceptable, and we needed to do better. When nursing tells leadership that one nurse should never have twelve patients herself when the standard is six to eight, leadership tells the nurse they just need to deal with it. Their answer is always the same. Leadership makes rounds with us to make sure we do the "right things" and say the "right things" during report. These are part of the system algorithm, so instead of inspiring us to have the heart of Christ, which would follow the principle of serving Jesus, which is the mission our hospital says they live by, they instead force us to follow a worldly system that is bent on making them money and serving false gods, such as FTEs, budgets, and control. It is an immoral system. We were told our whiteboards were not updated, and patients were reporting that nurses did not make rounds every hour, but it was two or more hours since they saw their nurse. Leadership tells us we need to do better. A patient complained to leadership that she did not get her pain meds that she asked for, then fell asleep with her baby in the bed with her, and did not see her nurse for two hours. Leadership questioned the nurse about this instead of showing accountability by acknowledging leadership is responsible for this nurse having a ten-patient assignment and not being able to deliver safe care. The confronting of a nurse was after my meeting with leadership that I had on August 17 that I will explain later in this letter. In the meeting, I specifically addressed the fact that nurses had to cut corners every day to care for patients because the patient assignments were too heavy, and therefore, nurses were not able to practice at their best as we were not following the safe staffing standards recognized by AWHONN. Why are we constantly hearing about whiteboards, more frequent rounding, and being forced to practice without autonomy? Instead of practicing with autonomy, we are expected to be robotic with specific words and actions to use when taking care of patients and expected to work tirelessly under distress, while the real issue is not being addressed. We need people before we need things. Yes, whiteboards are important but not without nurses to write on them. Yes, hourly rounding is important but cannot be done without enough nurses to see all the patients every hour. Giving directions on what to say and do during rounding is not what a nurse needs. We learn this in nursing school, and many of us have years, even decades, of experience in the field. The only reason more harm does not come to our patients is because of what is explained in Proverbs 21:30: "There is no wisdom, no insight, no plan that can succeed against the Lord." Our patients are protected by God, and we are vessels he uses to deliver care to people. We do not save lives. We do not create life or sustain it. This is all by the works of God, and we as nurses acknowledge that and understand our lowly position in the situation, if we are righteous at all. This is why we are not driven by fear of failure that comes from a weak mind, but instead, we labor in love and work from the heart, which is guarded by God. This is how it is possible to continue serving under the current circumstances honorably.

One of the principles recognized by the American Nurses Association for nurse staffing suggests that institutions must employ a culture of safety and must recognize appropriate nurse staffing as integral to achieving goals for patient safety and quality of care. Practiced principles are what creates a culture. The resulted environment of a nursing unit is established by what type of activity the institution practices over time. This is what creates a culture among those who are involved, all employees associated in the unit. RNs do have a professional and moral obligation to report unsafe conditions and inappropriate staffing situations that adversely impacts safe and effective quality of care. RNs should be provided with a professional nursing practice environment in which they have control over exercising authentic and appropriate nursing practice while maintaining autonomy in their workplace. I have explained to upper management after writing a safe care and CEO gram that our nurses must cut corners daily to get the expected workload completed. They have feelings of dread when coming to work, have trouble sleeping at night before scheduled shifts, and express feeling anxious about their assignments. I hear from many nurses, even seasoned nurses with decades of experience, that they cry during their shifts and have come close to walking off the unit and quitting. We go home with nothing left for our kids and husbands. We leave work and fight to preserve what dignity we have left. Some nurses admit they feel the need to drink alcohol after their shifts to calm down. Some overeat and indulge in all their favorite snacks and junk food just to take the edge off. Some nurses soak in the tub or take antianxiety pills to cope. Some take the long way home and make it just in time to tuck their kids in bed before getting the chance to cry out their frustrations after they were forced to work a twelve-hour shift and missed their little one's sporting event that night. The integrity of leadership is questioned when it is brought to their attention that the matrix we were given from corporate is worse than the one we were following before, and it further does not follow or support the AWHONN standards for safe staffing. Direct management is aware that the current matrix for staffing the unit is not suitable. Leadership still implements the matrix and has made no changes to our workload even though there are nurses available to work and even regularly scheduled nurses are canceled to keep the unit working under these harsh conditions to save the budget and to meet productivity. I wonder what those people in leadership are rewarded with to keep these numbers down. I use words like *budget* and *productivity* because these are words used to explain why the unsafe environment has not changed and been improved. What does profit sharing mean to this ministry? Who does this ministry serve? They say they serve Jesus, but I have studied God's Word my whole life and have a relationship with Jesus, and I am fully aware that this institution's actions do not reflect the attributes of Jesus. Is it not possible to work safely and be cost-effective? Talking in business terms, is it not productive to keep your nurses working at full capacity to deliver or produce good, safe care? If you do not take good care of your machines in a factory and they break down and need to be repaired or do not function at their best, is this not going to negatively impact productivity? Good productivity on the mom and baby unit would be nurses able to take care of their own families well at home, getting a good night sleep before coming into a facility they love being at. Good productivity would mean the nurses could come to work and take good care of their patients and stay focused on the job at hand. They would not be worried about the money needed to fix their cars or buy needed appliances or pay for their child's sporting events because the facility they work for would pay them a fair wage that covers costs of living. I see good productivity as nurses having time and energy to teach new moms how to be a confident parent by staying by their side, answering questions and assisting them with their new babies. I see good productivity in nurses teaching dads how to transition into the role of fatherhood by caring for their newborn while also being a supportive partner to the baby's mother, inspiring them to be leaders in their households. Reportedly, one of the biggest and most devastating crimes in America, and one growing at a fast rate is sex trafficking of our youth. Experts say the problem lies in the family unit at home because most kids are not kidnapped and dragged away by force, as many tend to believe. Many children are lured away by the trafficker when he gains trust by saying things that make the child feel special and attractive, wanted. Family units in America are weak. We have the opportunity and the honor to play a part in building the foundation of the family unit with these parents. We can give them tools to start out right and the confidence to build a more supportive and stronger family unit for kids in America if we focus more on authentic productivity. I see good productivity in sending a healthy mom and baby home in confidence that everything possible was done to promote stability, good health, inner strength, and family bonding while they were in our care. This kind of good contribution from our "business," the business of serving in the medical field, would be transformational and would positively affect America. This, sadly, we are not doing. Instead, we are working for the bottom line. Getting many patients in and out fast. We are working to have no interruption of the financial gain for all the working positions and leaders above direct patient caregivers. This is what productivity means to this institution. The proof is in the people. I saw leadership's true character when I met with upper management, as they claim to be honest and transparent with me but explained that they have never seen the mom and baby matrix and did not know what matrix we are operating under. This response does not support engagement, accountability, or responsibility. It represents poor communication between upper management and direct management. Through discernment, I could see, after speaking with leadership, that their distorted view of productivity trumped proper treatment of people, and this would explain a lack of ethics and civil-mindedness. I am beginning to understand why our unit is in such big trouble and why America is not the country it can be as I follow the trail of actions and words of our leadership.

The assignments we receive on mom and baby have created a toxic environment. This was brought to leadership's attention, and they responded by saying that this was concerning to them and warranted immediate response, and they took notes as if they were focused and engaged in the conversation. Nothing resulted, mimicking the results of all the times in the last several years that these same issues have been brought to their attention. They were actors. They were not concerned. A lack of trust has developed between the nurses and our leaders.

I have heard nurses say that maybe if we just lower our standards too, we will not be so upset with how our unit is being run. Our nurses take pride in their work ethic, but the heavy assignments, lack of ancillary services, and lowered standard have caused missed meds, poor reports given on new admissions, missed deliveries by doctors, missed or overlooked IV infiltrates, blood work being drawn on wrong patients, missed blood work, unsigned permits, vaccines given without consent to babies when this was not desired by the parents, patients going long periods of time in pain, misidentifying patients resulting from the poor planning of a bed coordinator and charge nurses who distract the nurses and aides by making several changes per shift of patient's rooms. They desire control and love to micromanage, and these positions should be removed and filled with people willing to do the groundwork with honor. Leadership has even resorted to harassing and bullying the nurses to discharge patients faster so they could admit the next one into the empty room. Leadership has encouraged nurses to rush patients into rooms that are not ready and even transported patients themselves to our unit and left them in the hallway to wait for their room to finish being cleaned and then set up, breaching policy and violating HIPPA. They have put patients into rooms with wet floors, putting the nurses and patient's safety in jeopardy. There is no time to chart on the discharged couplet or even set up the room or plan for the new patient before they arrive. Sometimes the new patient arrives with no report and is brought by a tech who knows nothing about the patient. It is becoming common practice to send patients over to postpartum from labor and delivery with no pain relief. Sometimes this is because the nurses say they do not have the needed supplies to deliver the pain med, such as a PCA pump. This is not an excuse to not follow through and delay patient care. Sometimes type 1 diabetics come to our unit without having an established insulin plan, causing their blood sugars to be unstable. Sometimes there are patients who are on a drug treatment plan and have been going to a clinic for rehab, but no orders have been put in for them to continue their drug rehab program in the hospital. All these examples are to show the poor quality of care that begins during the admission process in labor and delivery. The communication between doctors and nurses, nurses and patients, and nurses and nurses is poor. Cutting corners is regular practice because patient assignments are not appropriate. So now even when they have time to properly admit patients, they may not. Nurses are in rush mode often, and what you make a habit out of doing is what you're going to continue to do; even when you have time to get everything done, you may tell yourself you don't. These missed steps cause delay of care to the patients and extra and unnecessary stress on the postpartum nurse who is rushing to get the patient admitted to their unit with heavy assignments themselves because even when we have the staff, we are forced to cancel scheduled staff and work shorthanded to worship the budget. Sometimes nurses admit they did not call the doctor about an issue or admission orders because they just did not want to deal with them, referring to doctors who give nurses a hard time for calling them. Not only is this practice irresponsible, unsafe, and dangerous, but it sometimes causes problems to trickle all the way down to discharge, causing longer hospital stays for moms and babies. I questioned a senior leader on this, and she admitted she knew who I was referring to and said she realizes this as a problem. *Are you kidding me?* I thought. It's not a problem for me because I have made it known I do not tolerate being spoken to without respect from anyone, including doctors, and I am an advocate for my patients, so I call if it is necessary; otherwise, I handle my business however I can in my realm of practice. Knowing your worth is necessary in nursing, and you must acknowledge the power you have in your domain, or you will get taken advantage of, and so will your patients. Leadership has no excuse to allow certain doctors to worship themselves and abuse other members of the medical team. I always look out for other nurses who need to hear that they have worth and autonomy and must act on their patient's behalf.

There are standard principles suggested for the practice environment to ensure nurses' good health, well-being, and stamina, not only for them but for the prevention of fatigue-related errors that would affect the patient.

According to the American Nurses Association, the ratio of nurse to patient should be adjusted based on the patient, and this is a good baseline. The patient should come first. One nurse to six patients or one nurse to three couplets is the general standard for our unit, and even with this, years of experience of the nurses taking care of the patients and acuity of patients are considered. We should ask ourselves what our patients will need on a given day. For example, does a patient have a language barrier and need interpretation? Circumcisions take a considerable amount of time for the nurse, and sometimes a nurse will have three in one shift with eight or more patients in their assignments. Having a patient who requires social services can sometimes take up a lot of time for the nurse, especially on the weekends when social work is not available, and this responsibility is left to the nurse. These considerations are not accounted for by our leaders who staff us on a nurse-to-patient ratio of one to eight, one to ten, one to eleven, one to twelve, meaning one to four couplets, one to five couplets, and even one to six couplets at times. This is sometimes with no aide and no secretary, and we do our own work on our moms and babies including assessments, blood sugars, circs, ODHs, car seat challenges, and CCHDs. We have one nursery nurse, and she is responsible for admissions, and this is her main job along with getting report on every baby and being a resource of information. It was reported to me that one night there were several car seat challenges being done in the nursery. There were many babies and nurses in there all night, as tasks needed to be completed. The congestion caused the nurses to sweat, and they were complaining about how hot it was in there from all the activity, but they had no choice; they had to get the work done. The nursery nurse reported vomiting twice that night because of the working conditions on the unit.

The construction and setup of that nursery is not conducive to the amount of babies that it serves and to the nurses who deliver care.

Positive and healthy workplace culture is respected by the American Nurses Association, and it is suggested that to maximize safe patient care and quality outcomes, health care systems must recognize that in addition to safe staffing, they must provide sufficient interprofessional support and ancillary services. I understand that these standards are to be looked at on an individual basis, but I continuously hear excuses as to why we do not support standards. Our leadership has been asked to hire an LPN for the nursery to assist us with circs, blood work, and other types of baby care, but they refuse and will not acknowledge the importance of having ancillary staff in addition to RNs. Even our charge nurses have full assignments, often eight or more patients, so she is not available to be assigned these tasks.

A considerable change is now needed since our leaders have ignored the need to increase staff over time. Younger and smaller babies are now being taken on our unit. Detox babies are considered less intense than they were years ago but still need more attention and care than babies not born on drugs. This is not considered concerning staffing. We have more non-English-speaking patients on our unit than ever before, and these patients take a considerable amount of time to care for because of the language barrier. We have more tasks to be done on babies including blood sugars, CCHDs, and delayed baths or in-room admissions if moms choose this. We have more charting that is expected and more paperwork such as postpartum depression screenings along with discharging in one to two days as opposed to two to three days. None of this has been considered with how we staff the unit. It has even gotten worse over the years, more patients per nurse, in addition to the workload increasing. I have heard that the United States is the leader of the developed world in pregnancy and birth-related deaths of women. What I have described in how we rush women and babies out of the hospital only a day or two after giving birth and how we do not give our full attention to these patients while they are in our care must be seen as part of the problem, or we are just not being honest with ourselves.

    Accredited hospitals allegedly offer some of the best working conditions in the entire industry. It is the gold standard of quality care when it comes to patient and employee satisfaction. Nurses and patients gravitate toward these hospitals because of their supposed favorable working conditions. My research in this field led me to information put out by Magnet, AWHONN, ANA, AAN, and the Joint Commission. I realize how critical it is that God be involved for any of these standards and practices to be put in place. What good is theory without practice? These facilities should have low turnover rates and low vacancies. It should be a positive work environment. A few of the characteristics suggested of an accredited hospital are appropriate management style, quality of leadership represented, quality of care given to the patients, and an organized structure. It is suggested, and I agree, that in these hospitals, nursing leaders are visible, accessible, and committed to communicating effectively, fostering a professional bond, the important element of cohesiveness between floor nurses and leaders. The leaders are trusted and their employees experience job satisfaction, which results in patient satisfaction. My question is how in the world has my hospital, the one I explained in length, qualified for this accredited status? Is there something wrong with the evaluation process? Has the truth been covered up or distorted? I am at least $7 an hour underpaid for my years of experience and probably even more underpaid for my specific position. My wage does not match my market value and my years of experience in my field. There are others like me as well. I have been underpaid for years, but recently as inflation has made it tough on Americans, I was still overlooked for a raise. Management knew this and admitted it, but did not fight for me to get a fair pay. I believe that God is my provider, and I am committed to serving the community and have been loyal to God who has called me to continue to serve where I am. The question remains. Why am I not valued and my family not given a fair share of profit? The same respect of people's health being given by the organizations pushing the jab is also being seen in the hospital by leadership toward nurses and other health care providers. There is a sense of superiority seen in those at the "top" who believe they are the ones who matter and everyone else is just to be used to serve them and listen to their instruction. As a nurse, I believe in autonomy for myself and my patients.

 A few weeks ago, on August 17, 2022, I came into work and saw on the assignment sheet that I was getting pulled from my unit and sent to the labor and delivery unit to take care of overflow patients. As I looked, I could immediately tell that my assignment would be a nightmare, as is usually the case when we get pulled over there, and this alone creates anxiety on our unit. I have had years of experience being in charge and can easily see the difference between a fair, unfair, or completely unsafe assignment. I looked at my manager and said that my assignment was bad, that it did not follow the AWHONN standards and that it would be a terrible day for me and for the patients. She studied the assignment as if she had not seen it that morning or was not aware of the nature of it. She never changed it. Sometimes management will seem to justify their actions surrounding short staffing by running around and assisting nurses with little tasks. This is nice and appreciated, but this does not justify shorting the unit and is not considered a respectable way of troubleshooting when most of the time these difficult shifts can be seen coming. This would be the equivalent to putting a Band-Aid on a gushing wound. If the source of bleeding is not found and stopped, eventually, the patient will bleed out. I had been able to see this in too many forms in this hospital chain, procrastinating in doing what needs to be done to help people on so many levels.

Military training is similar in a lot of ways to nurse training. In battle, if an officer in high rank must pull his weapon and fight alongside his men, it is known that they have failed as leaders and are losing the battle. The outcome is, at that point, grim. We are in a constant battle on our unit, and our nurses are tired of fighting so hard all the time. Our leaders pat themselves on the back when they help us when we are drowning. They don't acknowledge the truth that they are in a constant losing state. Officers in the army who are of good character will acknowledge their soldiers in the field because they value their experience and hard work in the battlefield. The officers uphold principles and stay consistent in practicing their seven values: loyalty, duty, respect, selfless service, honor, integrity, and personal courage, and this way they can help those under them to develop leader attributes. High-ranking officers and soldiers in the field have a give-and-take relationship, and respect must be reflected by both. This is very similar to how the nursing unit should function.

The assignment I was given on August 17, 2022, when I was pulled to labor and delivery, was inappropriate, but nothing was done about it. I have spoken up for my coworkers in the past when I could and have adjusted the assignments when it was in my scope of practice, but it is a culture now to just suffer through the day because most of the time everyone is working in similar circumstances. Everyone is shortchanged, so you'd be robbing Peter to pay Paul by moving things around. I did not have an aide on the seventeenth, and I had four couplets. The first couplet was a vaginal delivery whose recovery was complete, but the baby was still in the room. The baby was not taken to the nursery and admitted, and report was not given to the nursery nurse, which is the normal and appropriate practice at our facility. The night-shift nurse just ran out of time to transfer the baby. Inconsistency with carrying out important tasks is becoming the norm now, and it is just overlooked. The permits were not signed, and the baby needed started on the blood sugar protocol after the blood sugar was found to be low. This mom needed to be admitted and needed all supplies set up in her room. I had to leave my patients in labor and delivery and transfer the baby to the nursery and give report before even starting my shift. Cleaning up after the last shift or cleaning up a disorganized transfer has become the norm, and this was not how I was trained, and it is not acceptable practice to me, which is why I and leadership do not see eye to eye. They know I have seen things from a more efficient and safer angle, and they know I expect this from them but am not getting it. I raise the bar; therefore, I am seen as a threat. I know I am not valued in this hospital, and I know they want me to move on. This discernment will be proven true later.

My next patient was a vaginal delivery less than twelve hours delivered who was a postpartum hemorrhage with an EBL of 950 ml. She was too tired to care for her baby from her delivery and blood loss, so she asked that the baby remain in the nursery until she could eat and have more strength. Her baby needed to be fed and was circumcised while it was in there, and thankfully, the nursery nurse knew of my assignment in the other unit and was able to assist with this, but most of the time, she would be busy admitting babies, and this would not be possible, and it would be my responsibility. This patient also needed to be admitted and needed her room set up with supplies. The circumcision was routinely not done until after the twenty-four-hour mark, but since we were rushing to get people moved along like they were products on a conveyer belt, we just kept moving. This is becoming a factory or mill instead of a hospital.

My next patient was a C-section that was twelve hours post-op. When I was getting report, the nurse said the patient had already been calling for a half hour for pain meds, but the nurse did not have a chance to get in there because she was busy with her other patient. This patient would need to be up with assistance and needed to be admitted to the room and the room set up with supplies. Her blood work was missed on night shift, so I had to draw it that morning, and it was not back for the doctor when she rounded. She was a first-time mom and needed help breastfeeding.

My last patient was a C-section, eight hours post-op, non-English speaking with suspected chorioamnionitis, had a temp, and was on IV antibiotics. She needed to be admitted to the room and needed supplies. She needed her Foley removed, blood work drawn, and up with assistance. The labor and delivery nurse told me in report that she had not seen this patient in hours because she was busy with her other patient. This patient was in so much pain that she could not ambulate with me when I tried to get her up at the scheduled time.

I had a meeting with upper leadership about this assignment along with writing a safe care report and a CEO gram to the president and was told that immediate changes needed to be made. Nothing changed.

On August 31, 2022, there were five scheduled C-sections. I had looked at the assignment at 3:00 p.m. when I was leaving and saw how bad things really were that day. Charge nurse had ten patients.

Another nurse had nine patients; she ended up with a total of twelve patients that day after two discharges and three admissions.

Another nurse had eight patients; one was deaf and Spanish-speaking only, a discharge, and had to restart an IV on a patient getting IV antibiotics, a circumcision, and two ODHs/CCHDs/blood sugars.

Another nurse had eight patients, two discharge couplets, and one C-section admission. She had a total of ten patients that day. Another nurse had eleven patients, and one of the moms had twins. She began with four couplets, and then the mom with twins was added to her assignment at 3:00 p.m., giving her the eleven patients.

Another nurse had ten patients. She had a baby under phototherapy with labs, another couplet with an ODH/CCHD/ blood sugar and was to be discharged, another couplet with no prenatal labs, another couplet that was a discharge, and an admission that had no bed, so she had to admit the patient and care for the couplet while they stayed in a room on the labor and delivery unit, splitting her between two units. This couplet later changed rooms and was moved and admitted to mom and baby. The baby was cold on admission and ended up having both a circumcision and a frenectomy.

On September 1, 2022, some assignments were as follows:

One nurse had seven patients, and one was to be a discharge but was having high blood pressure. Another was a C-section twenty-four hours post-op with twins, one in the NICU, one on the unit. She had a spinal headache and was getting treatment for it. Her baby had low blood sugar.

Her last patient was a C/S less than twenty-four hours.

Another nurse that day had a C-section less than twenty-four hours post-op, another C-section with history of gastric bypass who was having stomach issues, a new admission C-section who had a nicked placenta and had two units of PRBCs (packed red blood cells) in labor and delivery. She also had leukemia and had to keep her Foley catheter in for twenty-four hours. This was the admission she was given after discharging a different patient from that room. She also had a border baby (baby whose mom was already discharged.) She had nine total patients that day.

That day our leader pulled the breastfeeding consultant off her duties to work as a staff nurse. This left only one breastfeeding nurse to see about twenty-five or so breastfeeding moms by herself. The breastfeeding consultant who does not work on the floor on a regular basis had three couplets to start. She discharged two sets and got two admissions.

The charge nurse had seven patients. Two sets had no prenatal labs. One baby was put under phototherapy and had a circumcision she had to assist. Another baby had a circumcision she had to assist with. She had a discharge and lastly a border baby.

Another nurse had four sets of discharges and an admission that was non-English-speaking, for a total of ten patients that day.

Another nurse had a sixteen-year-old vaginal delivery, a C-section with twins that was a discharge, another set that was a discharge, and then a new C-section admission, for a total of nine patients that day.

Another nurse had two C-section couplets under twenty-four hours, a discharge set, and another couplet with a circumcision. She had a total of eight patients that day.

This day we had no nurse's aide.

These are some example assignments on our unit. It has been this way for so long, and the morale is low.

How in the world can nurses continue to function in this way? Bravo to my coworkers for weathering the storm. This is through God's grace and mercy that we strive through these shifts with fortitude and honor, but this should not be the way the day goes. Nursing must take a turn for the better.

First and foremost, we need to start following the AWHONN staffing standards for our unit. Why is there such a conflict between the standard way of staffing and the way our hospital staffs their unit, and why does our community and our state allow substandard care of people, nurses, and patients for the sake of making a profit? Usury is another principle that is being worshipped over goodwill in the medical field, and we need to acknowledge the truth of this.

We need a nurse's aide on every shift. We need an LPN or extra RN in the nursery to do labs, assessments, feedings, blood sugars, CCHDs, car seat challenges, assisting with circumcisions and frenectomies. We need a secretary at least until 11:00 p.m. every day. We need to expand our unit and nursery, and finally, we need to be a closed unit, independent of the labor and delivery unit. This is what we as nurses on the mom and baby unit are proposing. We expect change. We need change.

I am concerned about the short-term and long-term effects of the mental, physical, and emotional health of my coworkers. I do not hesitate to say that it is a shame that we as nurses are treated so poorly at our hospital. I have taken much time and effort to listen to my coworkers and, through conviction, have tried to explain in this letter to the best of my ability what must change on our unit. I refuse to lower the standard.

I had the chance to converse with my daughter Sabria during her final year at West Point Military Academy, who studied to be an officer in the army and a leader during her service on the civilian side. She is a born leader striving to live for something bigger than herself. We did not know of each other's meetings but were both meeting with leadership in the same week to discuss our passions in health care, her at West Point and me at my hospital. She had explained that as a daughter of a nurse and the oldest of six kids, she was able to learn and see over the years how the medical field's focus has shifted from quality patient care and respect of medical professionals to profit and productivity. However, the word *productivity* has been vastly misunderstood and misused. Authentic productivity would mean the delivery of safe and effective health care, delivered by a physically and mentally healthy, free, conscious, and well-compensated medical professional. She saw how this shift in focus has negatively affected and impacted the entire household of the families of patients as well as the families and households of medical professionals. She became passionate about making change at the leadership level and desires a position in med service. She said that after tearing her ACL during a basketball practice in her freshman year at West Point and then undergoing surgery, she had a really great team of doctors, including her surgeon, recovery therapists, and athletic trainers. She was able to gain perspective through this experience and was able to see that having proper care and attention allowed her to recover and become better than she was before her injury. She no longer saw her injury as a negative but was, instead, something that helped her grow. She was able to see that how patients are responded to and how leadership treats their staff who deliver care to patients will have either a positive or negative impact on patients and families, and this affects our country. Transformational leadership is a powerful tool. She was able to see the whole picture. She hopes to make a big impact, and she inspires me to do the same. God has opened my eyes to see but also has called me to act, to speak up and expect change and to also expect this in others. This explains true, authentic productivity and leadership.

I am not just a nurse. I am a wife, mother of six, published author, exercise and health enthusiast, promoter of free speech, and most importantly, I am a follower of Christ. I have a life outside of this hospital, and I live my life to inspire others to make change. You might say I am in the business to produce authentic leaders. I do not do business the way others do. I am not a user and abuser for selfish gain. I believe that all nurses are not just nurses, and I see them as individuals who have dreams, potentials, and unique gifts. They are good at many things, and we should encourage them to continue learning always and to become all they were meant to be individually.

They have responsibilities outside of the hospital that require energy, stamina, mental toughness; and they need to face these responsibilities without being completely depleted from their jobs at this facility. Please start to understand that these people, who serve, should also be served. This should be a give-and-take relationship. If this organization supported nurses and treated them as valued individuals, things would change all the way around. Please start investing better in the lives of those who serve at this facility every day. Just because I did not go back to school to earn a higher degree in nursing does not mean that I did not continue learning and that I do not deserve to be invested in. Just because this hospital offers tuition reimbursement does not mean they offer educational support or advancement to their nurses. I chose to embrace my talents in other ways, and I invested in myself in ways other than obtaining more college degrees because I personally did not see more college as a benefit to my career or my life at this time. If more college is desired by a nurse, support and encourage them, but it is not all there is and certainly is not necessary or even beneficial for every nurse to gain more college degrees. I have very special and unique qualities that I bring to this hospital daily, a very specialized skill set that directly comes from the investments and hard work I allowed God to build in me over the years. God continues to build me in ways that only he could, and I am thankful that I think outside of the box. We all, as nurses, deserve to be well taken care of and supported at work so we can go home and still have energy for ourselves, our families, friends, and other missions. Please decide to be better and truly support nurses and all medical professionals in ways that are beneficial and not just in ways that sound good in conversation or look good printed on paper or in reports. Nurses should not be put in a pigeonhole but, instead, should be valued and appreciated as free thinkers, creative, expert troubleshooters, and warriors with endless gifts and talents that don't begin or end with their nursing degrees, titles, or positions. We are people, God's people. Acknowledging this will change our country for the better.

Thank you for reading this and please consider making a change where you can. I am very hopeful that with so many great support systems involved here, change can come to our unit. God has taught me that sometimes our problems may seem like mountains, but even having a little bit of faith is enough to move mountains. Instead of seeing the budget as a stop sign, make the proper changes and ask God to expand the budget to make it go as far as it needs to go to take care of his people. I do this in my own life, and it does work. Jesus did not wait for there to be enough bread and manna to feed the five thousand people. He prayed over the food and told the disciples to pass it out. They were obedient to Jesus, and the five loaves of bread and two fish were enough to feed the five thousand people. Start living by faith to care for God's people. He still does miracles today, and he is our true provider.

We look forward to speaking with you to rectify these problems so we can better support and serve the community.

Me and my daughter Sabria connect and supported each other through our passion for change in the medical field.

Chapter 15

The Meeting

On September 27, 2022, I finally had my meeting. This meeting was set up to discuss the problems on our unit and my first letter, and included the three of us mom and baby nurses known as the "task force," and also in attendance were high, middle, and low-level leadership representatives, a few other nurses, and a human resources representative. I had prepared a second letter, a twelve-page paper, carefully and respectfully describing specific problems on the unit. After everyone introduced themselves, I said I would like to read the second letter I wrote. Immediately, the representatives for the company said that I was not to read my letter. They said that I could email them my letter but that I should not read it in this meeting because this was a time for everyone to talk and share information. I was told that they did read my first letter, in which I explained this was a collaborative approach, and the letter spoke for many. They continued to say nothing good about it and did not thank me for bringing these problems to light through the first letter. Instead, the human resources rep had a tone and said that I had listed lots of problems on the unit but did not suggest any solutions. So these leaders in this meeting would tell me a story, and I would listen. I listened with my heart, where the Holy Spirit lives. That is how I can identify deception and lies. I could already see this woman wanted me to do my job and hers as well. I told them that my letters were designed to present a collection of problems that all nurses on my unit talk about regularly and have talked about for years and there were clear solutions in both letters. I was still told "no," that I could not share the letter in that meeting. I was not allowed to speak of what I knew. They didn't want to hear my story, and this was the difference between us. We were told in this meeting that we could meet every two weeks and could come up with two topics at a time to discuss in these meetings. I let my coworkers have the floor, and they both brought up some topics. One of the leaders leaned back in his chair, folded his hands behind his head, and said, "It sounds like we have some homework to do." I just looked at him in dismay, wondering what in the world he thought we had been doing for the last six weeks. He said he read my letter, so why didn't he have any answers or suggestions? I had spent forty-plus hours already of my own time on this project and explained in much detail how this facility needed to change. I was very prepared for this meeting and yet was not allowed to have a voice. Now he suggested doing homework? Why was I even there? I looked at the clock knowing my daughter's volleyball game would be starting soon, and I gave up going to the game to come to this meeting. Now regretting the decision, as I sat quietly, not even given the chance to speak. My first letter prompted this meeting in the first place. We, the floor nurses, already did more than our share. We were the force behind these letters and this meeting, and we were led by God, protected, and fueled by truth. I was there on my wedding anniversary, September 27, and during my daughter's volleyball game, being mocked by the organization by being told that I cannot have a voice. I would have gotten up and left that meeting as soon as I was told I couldn't speak as I could already discern we were not valued, but my coworkers were there, and they were being brave and learning to use their voice and to stand up for what is right, so I stayed to support them as they listed some concerns and gave some suggestions, the same kinds of things that were talked about in both my first and second letter. These women were boldly speaking truth for themselves and the unit, and I supported this. I was humbled by God that day, and I chose to stay, listen, and support my coworkers. This supports transformational leadership.

One key point that I did choose to suggest that day was the mom and baby and labor and delivery units becoming closed and separate units. I asked if this was possible. Two of the "higher-level" leaders both said "no," that it would not be looked at. One leader asked what the benefits would be, and I gave the answer that it would relieve a lot of anxiety that our nurses have because they are not comfortable going to labor and delivery as their skill sets are strong in mom and baby, and this is where they function well and with confidence. We can function better in an environment that supports our own skill sets. Bouncing between the units causes confusion and chaos along with this being a field we are not strong in, and it is common to get unfair and unsafe assignments when getting pulled there. One leader quickly dumped the idea and said this would not work because the hospital needs to "put bodies where they need to put bodies." Hearing this really hit the nail on the head. Our concerns were not valued. Even though my coworker gave an example, in this meeting, of a hospital she worked at that did this, and this unit was well organized and successful, he still said it would not work, and he arrogantly claimed he knew this from his experience in other units he oversaw. I could now see that I was correct in believing that this facility does not value individuality in nurses but only views us as "bodies," forcing professional ambiguity in the workplace and refusing to let us function in our specific, gift-oriented, God-inspired domains. This was a confirmation that this concern that I specifically addressed in the letters I wrote before this meeting were validated by God, as he gave me proof by this man's statements, attitude, and body language as he responded to our concerns. This was why it was important for me to listen, not only to my coworkers but to the leaders as the hearts of these leaders were laid bare through their talk, attitudes, and actions. Truth, through transparency, was revealed in them because you can try to hide what you truly believe, but sooner or later, the light will be revealed in how you respond to others. The human resources representative laughed and said, "We do have a staffing problem." I looked at her and said that it was not funny, and she stopped laughing and said, "Yeah, you are right. It's not funny." We were asked by the same one who called nurses "bodies" if we would be willing to exchange an aide on the floor for an LPN in the nursery. This has been talked about before, and this would not support the acceptable nursing guidelines. I asked, "You mean rob Peter to pay Paul?" He said, "Yeah, exactly." We said no, as if this ridiculous suggestion even deserved a response. At the end of the meeting, one of the leaders said she wished we had more information to discuss, which I thought was interesting since I had a twelve-page paper sitting in front of me that I was not allowed to discuss. I had plenty of information to discuss, but they did not want the truth. This was the type of psychological abuse that was so obviously forced on nurses and how our efforts and existence were mocked by management. Then human resources said we could plan the next meeting but chuckled and said that one of our leaders (the one who called nurses, "bodies") had another vacation coming up, so we would have to plan around that if we wanted him to attend the meeting. He smiled, blushed, and chuckled proudly. I was unamused at their petty jokes and realized then that I wanted nothing to do with them professionally or otherwise. The Bible says that some people will have a form of godliness but will deny its power and to have nothing to do with them. So I understood here that it was considered acceptable by leadership for me to miss my daughter's game, spend my anniversary preparing and then attending this meeting, and spending the last several weeks working on this unit's problems in my own time using deductive and inductive reasoning to come up with solutions that were continuously overlooked by leadership, and getting paid a low and substandard wage while on the clock. I was still told I had to do "homework," while one of our leaders was busy taking another vacation. I decided right then I would not be attending any more meetings and did share this with the other members of the "task force." I will still work to bring change, but I will not spend time with people who have spent years collecting paychecks for jobs they are not doing as they continue to receive unmerited pay while turning a deaf ear to ineffective floor operations and worshipping the god of plausible deniability, believing in their unmerited position in leadership. I decided to move on to search for professional and devoted people who choose to obey God's command to love others. I did not submit my second letter to them. They made it clear they did not want to read it, and they obviously were not interested in the content since they told me to email it to them but provided me with no contact information in which to send it. I decided to send it directly to the corporate office but still received no response.

The next day my manager smiled during a huddle in the nurses' station and with a bubbly attitude mentioned those who had October birthdays and anniversaries that month. She mentioned a few people's names and said happy birthday. This fake front is what really stands out to me. While facing a battle on our unit and nurses admitting we are operating in a toxic environment, switching the focus to empty positivity is the method taken by our leaders. This is what I can easily call mental and verbal jujitsu. This tactic of finding a way to relate to people using circumstances or people who are close to them is mental abuse and a way to channel maleficent ideology. It is used to manipulate people into certain activity or behaviors that will suit the abuser's intentions. It can even be used in instances such as hostage situations. Trying to manipulate the mind is what people do instead of fighting the way God teaches. Resisting the devil is the true way to fight, and this verbal and mental jujitsu can be an evil tactic, which would be used on me while advocating there in the hospital and later in my life too as I continued to learn who my friends and enemies were. My wedding anniversary was the day before this huddle, and my birthday was in October, but I would not dare bring that up so I could continue being mocked by this establishment, which really does not care about these events in our lives but only pretends to, and not very convincingly. I remembered all those patients I took care of over the years, and this is how I give them a voice. I think of how they can no longer speak, but somehow God is giving me that power, and I will use it to bring respect to him and all the "Sleeping Beauties" of the world. I had to believe there was power that came from the bedside, and this is where I practiced as a nurse. This was my battleground. It was a way to channel God's love. This is how I love others, to be an advocate, to use what I have for good and for the glory of God. This is the heart of a nurse.

This is my family who inspired me and this was who I found myself fighting for.

Chapter 16

Continued Fight for Change: Letter 2

This is a similar copy of letter number two. I wrote this a few months after the first when problems on the unit continued.

> Dear leadership,
>
> Leaders are responsible for implementing change. They should be willing to promote an enthusiastic environment by positively influencing staff.
> I explained that AWHONN standards should be implemented that very day when it was made known to senior leadership that this was not being done. I explained that it was possible, even imperative, to remove the current matrix and to start following the standards right then and there. Great leadership requires a response to conviction. The experts needed to develop the standards for those leaders and institutions who resisted their own good conscience by putting profit and productivity before quality care of patients and hospital personnel. Senior leaders are responsible for strategizing. They are needed to set up plans that will overcome obstacles, ignite passion in others, and break through

walls of resistance. Supplying mid-level leaders with appropriate resources to execute the plan is vital for success. I am shocked at how many leaders I have been in contact with who are making money at this facility, while the nurses are being the true leaders, coming up with solutions to the problems and learning of ways to implement them only to be told they must do more and that we need to hold meetings around the leader's vacations.

This is a problem that we have realized is embedded at a higher level of leadership than our immediate manager's position. One person cannot be blamed for the condition of my unit. There is a certain type of behavior that has been embedded in these leaders to only pretend to listen and care but strategize ways to delay correct response to these convictions. Witnesses reported seeing one leader pulling a copy of my first letter to leadership out of a nurse's hands, in labor and delivery, while she was reading it, and throwing it in the garbage. Being confronted with truth of specific facts in the letter has shed light on the true opposition between our leaders and nurses. They are causing confusion and conflict on the unit and speaking about making changes but not actually changing anything. They are, in fact, resisting change. I began searching for the reasoning and rationale surrounding the resistance and negative attitudes in response to truth. Actions speak louder than words, and this is what supports transparency. By watching leadership's actions, their intentions become clear.

Leadership has been making rounds and calling the unit to ask us how things are going on the unit when they cannot be physically there. Implementing evidence-based best practice and executing properly devised plans are what brings change and yields healthy results. Why has a proper matrix and acuity grid that supports AWHONN standards not been drawn up and executed by our management? Instead, rounds are being made, information gathered, and meetings scheduled, making it look like attention is being put on the issues. I provided plenty of information and assignments in my last meeting two weeks ago, yet the high-level leader decided, as part of the plan for change, to ask the mid-level leader to provide her with copies of the assignments. Meeting with the mid-level leader to strategize and put plans into action and then executing those plans would have been a more appropriate approach and would have been a very quick and timeless response. The mom and baby nurses provided leadership with a very detailed description of our assignments and retrieving more should have taken a couple minutes. Does our leadership have what it takes to interpret assignments and to decide what is safe and what isn't when compared to the standard? Why the delay? Why is acuity and the business of the unit not recognized when making assignments? Without conviction, simple obstacles can become permanent barriers to success.

What is typical of our leadership is making the assignments and unit look a certain way right before a visit from the state, and we have been expecting a visit, so the assignments do look somewhat better, not what they should be, but better than usual on paper. Even still, it has been a struggle to get through the last two weeks, and I personally had some shifts that had me desiring to find a new job. Nurses admit to being told that when a very popular and prominent accrediting organization came to evaluate our hospital, they were not to talk to this agency about staffing. What was leadership implying? If staffing was good and something to be proud of, wouldn't that be something to mention to the accrediting organization? If our unit is functioning well and according to the standards, why do we need to prepare for the state coming, and why are we asked to not be transparent and forthright with details of how our unit runs? Why was I asked to wait before sending my letter out to the state so that my hospital could make some changes first? The admission of problems has been made, but what we keep hearing in meetings is that these changes take time. Why the stall? This is typical of our institution. Our unit has asked for these changes for several years, and nothing has improved. In fact, the conditions have worsened over the last eight years.

I remember, at a time we were busy, bringing a patient to another unit to open a bed for a recently delivered postpartum patient. A med-surg nurse would assume care of my patient who was stable, and it was decided she would finish her stay on that unit. The med-surg nurse said to me that she knew nothing about OB patients, and it was obvious that she was not comfortable with taking care of the postpartum patient but would do it because nurses do what they are told and muscle through the situation even when it's tough or out of their comfort zone. The patient and the nurse seemed apprehensive about this transfer. This creates uneasiness in every party involved, including myself, as my goal is to establish trust with the patients. Trust is lost as the patient is dropped off on another unit because we do not have room for her anymore. It is especially hard on the patient who already is uneasy because her baby is in NICU (neonatal intensive care). We should be providing stability and solidarity at such a time of uncertainty, when she has more questions than answers. Another patient complained that she did not feel comfortable being put on a unit with so many sick people when her baby was in NICU and was susceptible to infection. This does not support best practice and should not be viewed as an appropriate plan or way of managing our department. We also run the risk of other units not being available when our census is up, so this plan is unreliable. These units are not equipped with a nursery or OB supplies. Only patients whose babies are in the NICU can be placed on these units, so it is a plan with limited options.

    I am focusing on specific and immediate changes that need to be made, which directly affect patients on the mom and baby side from admission to discharge. The fact that mom and baby and labor and delivery are always being thought of as connected units creates a constant weakness to each unit individually and the whole maternity department. There are major problems on both sides that need attention, and separating the two units has many benefits. Focusing on mom and baby problems independently is one benefit. Staffing our own unit rather than bouncing nurses back and forth between units provides dependability of staff, confidence in nurses, accountability between nurses to support the team, a sense of security for nurses, and promotes continuity of care for patients. Each department has nurses who are very specialized, and having them pulled to either side discourages them and does not support their true passion. Authentic leaders develop conviction through knowledge obtained by research and experience and use these developed qualities while maintaining professionalism in the workplace. They observe members of the team and identify their passions. Leaders with passion can persuade and inspire others to not just have passion but to ignite the fire inside them and to be effective in making this attitude contagious to others. This action results in a filling of the unit with genuine, conscience-guided, passionate nurses who care with heart, not merely supporting corporate compliance. The unit should have a shared goal together but should work in an environment that encourages and guides them to achieve personal goals and growth as well. This does not only mean climbing the corporate ladder or gaining enough college education to branch into the private practice spectrum. You cannot teach experience. Experienced nurses are gems, and they should be considered an asset to the team as they do a most important job of bedside care. Retention of experienced nurses is a problem at this facility, and leadership claims we must figure out why. The problem is in the refusal to acknowledge truth. I represent truth and, therefore, am meeting much resistance, and I can foresee that I will not be considered valuable or an asset to the team. I know I will be encouraged to leave my job soon whether directly or indirectly because I'm not robotic. I work under conviction of the Holy Spirit. I knew that when I began this mission, my job would be at stake, and people said they feared for me, but when you believe in truth, all else is sacrificed. I am not ashamed of standing up for what is right, and that will set me apart. It is a risk I am willing to take because I know who holds my future. If everyone did this, there would never be a threat on our freedom; there truly never is anyway.

This week on day turn, we had a nurse from labor and delivery pulled to our unit, and then they called her back to labor and delivery at 10:20 a.m., leaving our unit understaffed and our nurses over the limit on patients, according to the standard. We should be handling our own staffing so we can be responsible for filling our own positions and better manage the workload for the entire shift and not depend on people who commonly leave our unit to return to their own at the drop of a hat, leaving their assignments to be divided among the staff, further disrupting the unit, causing confusion and chaos. This week we also had mom and baby nurses pulled to labor and delivery when they could have been utilized on our unit, working in the nursery or taking patients off the higher acuity assignments. This sharing of staff is viewed by the hospital as a positive because it saves on labor costs and supports the budget. Meanwhile, it shortchanges patients and staff, therefore putting profit over people. My goal is to mitigate maleficent ideology that has contributed to the poor mental health of nurses, which supports a devaluing system of those called to serve at the bedside. Canceling nurses has saved the hospital plenty of money on our unit and other units, and this should be looked at and evaluated, possibly by support outside of this "ministry," which may need to enforce regulations that prevent the act of putting productivity before the needs of hardworking Americans and ultimately putting patients at risk. This sharing of staff is something our hospital brags about, and it is nothing more than a display of empty charity and the corruption of good character. It causes leaders to just see bodies instead of valuable individuals with specific skill sets and talents.

    On September 15, one of our nurses on mom and baby had six patients. One couplet was in COVID isolation, which should be considered high acuity. She had another couplet, who was a C-section from the fourteenth and then a couplet on antepartum who was a vaginal delivery under twenty-four hours postpartum, who was on a magnesium drip for high blood pressure. This mom is a high-acuity patient who would fall under the one to one ratio, not six to one. This nurse was distressed about her assignment, and one of our leaders was on the unit that day and made no changes to the assignment or even made mention of it to the nurse who had the assignment. This nurse was not even considered properly trained by our facility to care for a patient on a magnesium drip because she had not completed her orientation in labor and delivery. This orientation is just a way for nurses to be able to be used in labor and delivery but does not make them completely equipped to do the job confidently and with good experience and expertise. A mom and baby nurse who gets pulled to labor and delivery occasionally never develops experience enough to feel confident working in that environment. A labor and delivery nurse and mom and baby nurse are completely different, and both units are very busy specialized areas of our facility. The units need to be separated for both to operate optimally. AWHONN standards recognize a nurse's years of service in a field as being an important factor when making assignments, and this should be considered on our unit. This was not the first time this nurse had an assignment like this, and it was brought to the manager's attention before with nothing being done about it. This nurse was split between two units, and this is common practice in our department. Why was one of our nurses pulled to labor and delivery that day? No one should have been pulled to labor and delivery in the first place, but why was she not given the mag patient so the other nurse could have had a lighter, more appropriate assignment? The nurse who was pulled did have many more years of clinical experience than the other nurse, and yet the nurse with lesser experience had the more intense assignment. None of these things are considered by our leadership. Pulling our staff to labor and delivery causes stress and uneasiness. There are many nurses who choose to float in the hospital and even float from one hospital to another. This is a specific type of person who has very specific personality traits and acquires specific skill sets to do this well. To force nurses to float against their will, when they are uncomfortable with doing so and do not have the appropriate personalities or well-practiced skill sets to do this well is harmful to nurses and dangerous to patients. I and the other nurses have mentioned this repeatedly, over the years, but honest nurses at this institution are not heard. This behavior does not support strong, supportive, empathetic leadership, and yet I have witnessed it all the way to the top at this facility, which is why I am reaching out further, even writing this book in hopes that the message influences change.

Ephesians 2:10 says, "For we are God's handiwork, created in Christ Jesus to do good work, which God has prepared in advance for us to do."

We should not be dishonored by being thrown from this unit to that, but we should have autonomy as God gives us the right to decide with him what kind of work we choose, and if we choose to be a mom and baby nurse or a labor and delivery nurse and we work hard to become specialized in the field, this should be honored by the hospital. I have halted the writing of my next book, skipped out on decorating for fall, missed out on playtime and events for my kids, and left some household chores behind to prepare for these meetings with management because of my dedication to God and obedience to his call to action, which outweighs anything and everything else in my life. I am purposeful to practice integrity and to make it represent who I am. I have taken the time to transmit my convictions to others in this organization, and after listening to the nurses, I demonstrated knowledge, wisdom, and discernment in order to understand the reasons, rationales, and benefits of a targeted course of action that yields success and growth of our unit and chose to recognize the value of nurses and patients. But according to leadership, I am just a per diem nurse who does not deserve to be paid for my years of service and am not recognized for what I can and do bring to the unit. I and my coworkers are the ones concerned with these matters and reflecting after each day to see why the day did not flow well. I have studied my unit and researched to help leadership make changes, but in no way are my efforts and information being recognized, and I am in no way being compensated for my experience and expertise by the institution, and I am only asked to do more. I am doing much of this work on my own time, after work, between my shifts at the hospital, and on my off days. Procrastinating is to make a mockery of God. Labor and delivery and mom and baby both need and deserve change.

Being a true leader means you do things without anything expected in return, but this can also be abused. My family understands this, and we support each other and have a strong family bond as we all strive to be influential in the world around us, but that does not give this hospital the excuse to challenge my efforts and disrespect my time, energy, and response to conviction, abusing the very grace given them by God to even be in the leadership positions they are in. While we, the nurses, are investigating and strategizing, leadership is planning meetings, rounding and revisiting old ideas instead of executing the plans. This is a problem in this institution. Too many meetings and no execution. Aren't there people in this hospital getting paid and accruing vacation time to do this very job? How has this institution purposefully integrated our unique gifts and talents into our specific domains? Is it not to be a goal at this facility to know what our purpose in this life is, since this institution claims to follow Jesus? Leadership should have made the proper, God-inspired plans to strategize an appropriate plan of action that highlights their staff's specific strengths and supports growth. Instead, they revisit goals from the past that they never implemented and bring these plans to the table again. Recirculating ideas over the last eight years has done nothing good for our hospital and is a waste of valuable time. As God has qualified me, I have explained at length why change has not happened and why our unit has been in trouble for so many years. We are not bound or limited on purity. Why hasn't the hospital invested in becoming pure, for the sake of others?

Jeremiah 29:11 says, "'For I know the plans I have for you,' declares the Lord, 'plans to prosper you and not harm you, plans to give you hope and a future.'"

The mom and baby nurses have concern for the physical structure of the unit. The mom and baby unit needs to be expanded with more beds available along with remodeling the nursery to make it more suitable to care for the babies we serve. This expansion needs to be done on the same unit to prevent nurses from being split between units. There is an area across from our break room that could possibly be utilized as an area of expansion, but according to our leadership, it will cost $30 to $40 million, and that this is not an option. Why are unsafe options considered, but options that cost money but will be safe are not considered? Does our "ministry," not have the funds to do what is necessary for our unit to function optimally? I asked leadership if this was something I needed to ask our corporate leaders about, and they said no, that these were issues we should handle at the level we are at, but I am not seeing enough faith in our leaders to make the proper changes. I asked a high-level leader if she was coming to the meeting on September 27, but she said she could not make it because she had other meetings. The twenty-seventh is my nineteenth wedding anniversary, but I am committed to this unit and to my coworkers and have hope in bringing change. I asked my husband if he was okay with me attending the meeting on this day, and he said yes and told me he supports what I am doing. To some people, love means giving of yourself, and one who truly believes in love and its power encourages the instillation of this belief in their family as well, strengthening the family unit. Faith means the assurance of things hoped for, the conviction of things not seen. Faith is a necessary attribute of great leaders, and without faith, hope and conviction, leadership will not be effective but, instead, will slow or stop progress, prevent success, and will make it impossible to be trusted by staff.

On September 14, I had an assignment of six couplets. Right off the bat, this may look good if one is not able to interpret assignments and only looks at numbers, which is the common practice at our institution. One patient was a one-day postpartum vaginal delivery. Another patient was a one-day C-section patient whose baby needed ODH/CCHD/blood sugar. Another patient was a vaginal delivery, and it was discharging day.

My discharge patient only spoke K'iche', which is a rare dialect, and translators of this language are hard to find. K'iche' patients take up a considerable amount of time and should be considered a high-acuity patient. It is sometimes difficult to get an interpreter for this language and on night shift, it is nearly impossible, so no discharge teaching or communication was done on night shift. Why has this not been addressed by our leaders? When the leadership of our country welcomes people from other countries, at high numbers, they should provide what is needed for them to thrive here. This is being understood by authentic leaders in our country, and we can do our part at this institution by giving these patients the adequate time and staff needed to care for them. Nurses should not have to pay the price for poor leadership decisions in America. Poor leaders will not know the weight of their decisions until these patients are in their backyards or in their direct care, which we see happening now in society, and so-called leaders are now calling this a crisis in our country. It has been a crisis for others for a while now, but only leaders involved with their team and who have empathy will understand this. Our leaders in this institution should have known the influx of these types of patients would require more time and energy from our nurses, and this higher acuity should have been considered. We have been seeing more and more immigrants who do not speak English but also have other barriers associated with their culture that are presented during their hospital stay. Included in these barriers would be the idea that since we so openly invite and encourage people to come to this country and give to them freely on so many levels, the false sense of security and entitlement develops. This invites a trust of the system that was established by selfish intentions. This then puts pressure on the nurse who is encouraged by the system to get patients out of the hospital fast, not because this will benefit the patient but the business. These patients do not live in this country as we do. The lines are blurred for nurses concerning these patients, and this puts the nurses in a vulnerable situation. Many of these patients cannot read or write at all, even in their own language. I have wondered how they drive their new baby home from the hospital when it is impossible to drive a car legally in this country without a driver's license. We send them home anyway. Many cannot even make their own doctor's appointments, know how to get formula, or even understand how to use a car seat. The list goes on and on. It is obvious most times that these patients have not been living the same way as Americans, so how do we hold them to our country's standards and policies, say in the hospital setting? We have different cultures and ways of doing things in this country, and this coincides with policies and procedures at the hospital when communicating with these people. It is an automatic stressor to have this kind of patient in your assignment when the work involved is not accounted for in the assignment and when the quality of care is poor at best in these situations. What are we implying by allowing these patients into the country but are not willing to give them the attention they deserve as human beings? What are the intentions of this kind of activity? It comes down to this: how do you value people? If you do value people, you do what is best for them before worrying about making a profit for yourself. The profit is in the giving of good-quality care to God's people, and this is what this organization, state, and country refuse to recognize.

I began discharge instructions with this patient but lost connection with the interpreter through the iPad before finishing. When I tried to reconnect, I was called to the nursery to do a circumcision with the doctor. I left this room to assist with the circumcision, but right before administering the lidocaine into the baby, the OB doctor was called to a delivery in the labor and deliver unit. I left the baby with the nursery nurse and went back to discharging in the K'iche' room and began to try to connect with an interpreter again with the iPad. I turned the iPad on, but before I could make the connection, I was again interrupted and called back to the nursery to assist the doctor with the circumcision as his patient was not ready to deliver, after all. He tried to save time by running back and forth from one patient to the next, and the whole system gets kinked up this way. I assisted the doctor with the circumcision, and then I returned to the K'iche' room again to complete her discharge instructions. My day was tough and with unnecessary stress and interruptions. Our unit needs a nursery nurse who can perform tasks like circumcisions and blood work. My assignment was high acuity, and this should have been considered with staffing. Acuity and ancillary staff, along with proper nurse to patient ratios, is what AWHONN standards consider. Confusion and chaos lead to mistakes and disconnected lines of communication and is not consistent with running a cohesive team. The devil is the author of confusion.

On September 21, two safe cares were written concerning my patients. This happened after I left at 3:00 p.m., and things went downhill. I began the day with six patients. One was a discharge who needed her teaching completed and had a baby who needed a circumcision that day because the patient wanted to leave the hospital a day early. She planned to leave after 8:00 p.m. when the baby's twenty-four-hour blood work was completed.

I moved on to my next patient who was a C-section from the night before. She was twelve hours post-op when I assumed care. She was a type 1 diabetic and saw an endocrinologist who regulated her indwelling insulin pump. She told the nurses in labor and delivery that her endocrinologist needed to be consulted so he could adjust her pump after she delivered. Reportedly, the doctor told the nurse no, not to put in the consult, so no consult was ever put in before her C-section. I had the patient for day turn the next morning, twelve hours after delivery. This was too long for her to go with no attention paid to this issue. Her blood sugars were stable at this point, but she was concerned about her pump needing to be adjusted and rightfully so. At this point in my career, I am bold. You cannot learn boldness. It is a state of being that develops through teachings from experience. It only develops if one is willing to acknowledge truth. I called the OB to tell him I was consulting the endocrinologist, and he told me he did not know the endocrinologist wanted to be consulted. I don't play into these silly games anymore. I was just trying to get down to business in getting my patient proper care. If someone has an indwelling insulin pump that is regulated by a specific specialist, wouldn't any doctor be aware that these settings would need to be readjusted after a woman gives birth, and this specialist would need to be on board with the patient's care? Wouldn't a nurse who was properly trained and supported by leadership have autonomy in being the patient's advocate and consult this specialist even if the doctor said no? So when a doctor responds to me with such disregard for my patient, my intelligence, my years of experience, and my very existence, I do not fold into their schemes. I won't come down to that level. I just act in love and boldness and respectively move in the right direction. After I told the OB I was calling the specialist, I then did just that and consulted the specialist, and they said they would be in to adjust the pump.

I assisted with the circumcision on my other patient and then got a new admission, a vaginal delivery from that morning. After admitting her, I initiated high-intensity phototherapy and a Bili blanket on one of my babies, and as I was finally leaving and giving report to the next nurse at 3:00 p.m., my diabetic patient said she did not feel well, and her blood sugar was low according to the reader on her chest. Her blood sugar had remained stable all day, but now, it had finally tanked, which was bound to happen since initiative was not taken sooner by the doctor to consult her specialist and get her pump adjusted. A nurse with experience knows the importance of being bold because time is of the essence with patients like this. This is not respected in my facility, and nurses should be willing to fight for their patients from the very beginning of their stay. College credits cannot teach experience, boldness, integrity, and critical thinking. We got her some juice, and the other nurse took over care, as my shift was over. It was reported to me that her endocrinologist, whom I consulted earlier in the day, came to see her around the same time as a rapid response team was called on her because they could not get the patient to come around, and she quickly became very drowsy and could not respond appropriately to the nurse, even after treating her low blood sugar. She ended up having high blood pressure and needed to be treated for that as well, as her body responded to the drastic drop in blood sugar, which affected other systems in her body. This was all related to the delay of care she received on admission when her endocrinologist was not consulted to adjust her pump. She could have ended up in critical care with other issues if this went on much longer. It was abuse of the patient. She had needs that were identified as being urgent, and they were not dealt with by the medical team. I spoke to the endocrinologist personally the following day to see how his patients could be cared for better in the future concerning this issue. He told me he should have been consulted before the patient even went to surgery. This makes perfect sense and should have already been an established understanding by our leadership, but I was making sure to confront this issue since leaders were not willing to make the change before this incident happened. He was very willing to be a team player and respond to patients, but the hospital needed to communicate better, and this started on admission. Why are we fighting for these very foundational principles to be part of the discipline of this facility? These patients being seen by endocrinology for diabetes need consults put in on admission, before they even have their babies. I reported this to labor and delivery leadership who said they would let the nurses know. This is not the first time something like this happened, and it would continue if proper changes were not made. No action was taken last time I had a diabetic patient like this, even though a safe care was written. Confronting those involved in the delay of care is necessary to make change for these patients, specifically doctors who choose to not consult appropriate specialists for their patients and who do not encourage autonomy in nursing. It is a pride issue because some doctors just do not like collaborating with nurses concerning patients. Why do we even write safe cares if they are not addressed and the problems not solved? The system is faulty. Reporting back to the state that you made changes that you never made is inexcusable.

 I spoke to this diabetic as I had her the following day as a patient. She was an LPN herself, and she was disappointed in how things transpired during her stay. I let her tell me her story, and I listened. She reported that she told every labor and delivery nurse she encountered that her endocrinologist needed to be consulted to adjust her pump, and no one listened. There was no reason for what happened the day before with her sugar dropping and then her blood pressure going up. She said she felt the doctor was upset with her for things she brought up during her pregnancy and the fact that she was questioning him on some things. She said he oversaw her going home, and she wanted to discharge a day early, and after he did not have concern or consider her needs or respect her wishes concerning the consult, she figured he may not let her go home either, even though this is what she wanted. She thought that he would not respect her wishes. She shook her head and looked down at the bed. I gave her support and explained that

I was sorry for what she encountered. I encouraged her and let her know I was available to help her in any way I could. This story is an example of the toxic environment that I worked in on the daily. This poor treatment of patients and nurses is exactly what feeds the negative culture on our unit. It breeds substandard care. The nurses from labor and delivery had told me that they asked the doctor to put in the consult, but he refused, and his story was that he didn't know the consult needed made, which is ridiculous because any doctor should know this without a nurse telling him. Plausible deniability doesn't work to give an excuse for ignoring obvious core principles in your practice. He has this reputation of causing confusion and making things difficult, but this kind of evil can easily be extinguished if you fight with truth. He cannot tell me no, and he knows that because I laid the law down on that concept. I take care of my patients, and I will do what is best for them. Nurses need to stand up for what is right, and the doctors need to know they will. This is what stops that kind of evil. The hospital shares this evil, and that is why they let this go on and why I knew they did not appreciate my boldness. They didn't have it, and it can't be borrowed; it must be built within by God, and they knew they weren't willing to trust him in that process.

    Plausible deniability was alive and well on these units, and I was tired of having to blast my way through all the chaos, pride, and control freaks in order to properly care for patients. The lines are made blurry for nurses, and I know this is experienced in other units and hospitals all over the country.

THE VOICE OF TRUTH

Nursing in America is reported to be a leading career for depression and suicide. Nurses are burned-out, overworked, and underpaid. They must come to work ready to fight and not just against sickness and disease but against the maleficent ideologies of corporate compliance and self-worshipping medical professionals. Nurses express leaving the hospital in a fog with nothing left for the lives waiting for them at home. More studies are being done to see how the nursing environments could be less toxic, but if greed from the business owners running the hospitals does not get extinguished, this will continue. Why is my hospital chain building new hospitals and buying out other offices and hospitals without spending the money to fix problems in their current establishments? Why are they saying they don't have the money but still making financial gains? I had a very busy assignment that day I just described. I had eight patients and high acuity with cultural barriers, mistakes, and mismanagement by doctors and nurses that I tried to rectify during my shift. To add to this, there was only one nursery nurse, so all the work for the babies was on me as she would take charge of admitting babies. My goal was to self-reflect after that shift because quite frankly it was a disaster. Our unit needs to slow down. The nurses are distracted on our unit by having to do it all—collect data, notify proper staff when problems are revealed, and attempt to make multiple changes to this unit and give good quality care as well. It is hard to backtrack and try to fix what was not done appropriately during the admission process or on other units or during the patient's pregnancy before we get patients on mom and baby.

Sometimes we don't receive proper histories and blood work from the physician's office, which is necessary information to treat the patients. They know this is an ongoing problem, but since the nurse is the one to fix it and the patient is the one who gets blood work redrawn, the leaders don't care. There needs to be better evaluation of patients, prepartum, so they can be well established with a plan, postpartum. We must have better focus. Immigrants should be set up with classes to learn the culture, language, and flow of the process of having a baby here; and they can also learn how to use car seats, make doctor's appointments, and obtain driver's licenses to be safer on the roads. These are suggestions I only saw after being confronted with some negative experiences that could have been avoided. We are just flooding America with foreigners but not taking any responsibility for this. Staff nurses are the ones giving direct care to these patients and can see how problems develop because they spend time with these patients. The nurses need to be listened to. Long-term goals would be for these patients to thrive and to take responsibility for themselves using their voice effectively and understanding their role in their own health care. Of course, if these people learn to take responsibility for themselves, certain organizations will lose money, and because greed and financial gain are put before the health and well-being of people, this may not be looked at. Why would they want patients to have autonomy? That would take control away from the leaders, and they would not need to be depended on or trusted. We should appreciate and respect immigrant's own cultures, but we need to take responsibility to teach them American culture so that both cultures can be integrated to best care for them while they are in an American hospital and so they can function well and with confidence in the community, however long they are in America. We cannot, as nurses, be expected to do all of this in the one to three days that they remain as patients in the hospital after having a baby.

We should take care of people with integrity and pride and provide quality health care that will follow the patient long term, and this should be established during their office visits before delivery, but from what I am hearing from doctors and nurses, patients are rushed out of the office as well. The new way of seeing patients in the office is to limit time of the appointments. Things are being overlooked, and this negatively affects their hospital stay. We should be protecting our nurses, not setting them up to fail. People should be adaptable and able to have a healthy way to be tough on transition. Whether that means visiting another country, having a baby, or dealing with the diagnosis of a health condition. Just as God gives us immunity at birth to protect us against disease, he also gives us ways of facing other forms of adversity and gives us all we need to overcome and conquer. Support should be given to help patients to transition appropriately and with dignity. It is our institution's obligation to take this information into account and to make decisions daily to facilitate proper organization and flow to the unit and to hold a higher standard as Americans, but they do not take this seriously. We can do much to help this, including expanding our unit and decreasing patient assignments. We should be hiring more nurses and having available staff who will have time to spend with these patients while they are in the hospital under our care, teaching, offering support, carrying out duties. We cannot start the shift out with the bare minimum and expect to perform at a high standard. Nurses are spread too thin, even though the numbers on paper at times look good at first glance. The goal of good quality health care has gone out the window. I have begun to understand that God is calling me out to lead. I desire to find myself in a program that offers people quality health care that would benefit mind, body, and spirit.

I was seen a few months ago in the urologist's office, seeking treatment for a flare-up of a condition called chronic cystitis. The nurse practitioner said she sees a lot of nurses with this condition because nurses do not drink enough water or empty their bladders enough at work. I continue to struggle to keep this condition under control as it is associated with much pain and discomfort and can be completely debilitating if it gets out of hand. I work hard to stay on a strict diet and do specific exercises to prevent flare-ups. I am also looking into more natural treatments and possible cures for this condition which I am seeing results in, and it is looking promising even though it is considered by the medical field to be a non-curable, chronic condition. It is counterproductive when hospital administrators make rounds to make sure nurses do not have drinks at the nurses' station. This is to cut down on germs? It is ridiculous to believe that this rule is keeping nurses safe when the reality is that it is literally causing chronic health conditions. The hospital has been hurting nurses for years, and it needs to stop. We go many shifts without taking breaks because we are understaffed. I was canceled this week and made to stay home without pay while one of my coworkers had eight patients, and there was no nursery nurse to help because she was busy admitting babies. This is interesting to me since the head leader told me that the reason we do not have more nurses to follow the standard is because nurses are hard to find. How hard am I to find? I was easy to find when told to stay home instead of coming in for my scheduled shift. This is an example of their double standard. I could have been utilized in the nursery or to make the assignments at a safer acuity. The nurses may have started with six patients apiece, but with only one nursery nurse, the charge nurse having a full assignment and acuity was not looked at; this still does not follow the standard. Sometimes charge nurses, being on the unit with assignments, cannot view the day objectively. It is easy to think if their assignment is good and their day is flowing, then everyone's day is going well. This is why the manager should be making rounds consistently throughout the day to objectively make changes as needed, but this is only if the manager can interpret assignments and has support from upper management to follow the standards with conviction. I cannot say how many times I heard someone say, "Well, we worked short, so the next shift could work short too." So much is wrong with this statement and does not support good teamwork. Again, the culture needed to be changed. The standards get lowered as people accept the unacceptable.

  Recently I worked on a day turn. We worked with full assignments and no aide. Another nurse said she worked three shifts in a row with no aide. Our leader made rounds to check on patients and made sure we were doing our jobs, filling out whiteboards. This facility operates in a backward approach. Maybe our patients would be satisfied if someone made rounds to pass water and give patients supplies instead of asking how their day is going and if their nurse is coming in their room every hour. This seems like common sense, but apparently, it is not common. If our leader is doing what she is told to do, who is responsible for this backward behavior? Would it not be the one above her? So why is my boss getting heat for the way this unit is operated? I am not distracted in this, and I am not fooled as to what is going on. We have been programmed for so long to just manage with less. In fact, there was a postpartum nurse this week who got pulled to labor and delivery, and their call nurse was sent home. This nurse was working 7:00 p.m. to 7:00 a.m. and got a five-patient assignment. One patient was on a magnesium drip and another patient was still recovering from delivery. The nurse did not make it in the room to see her magnesium mom until 9:00 p.m. because her assignment was too heavy. Her assignment forced her to break protocol, but labor and delivery charge nurse thought this assignment was appropriate. I respect nurses on all the units, and I understand that this has become just the way things are done, but now is the time to wake up and realize that we have a choice and an obligation to make good choices concerning staffing.

  Many incomes of nurses have dropped considerably over the last two years as a result of being canceled to save money on the budget. Nurses also have not gotten due raises over a considerable amount of time. The workload has only increased. I am sure the hospital stays in good standing if productivity is met even though the nurses and patients are paying the price for a business being "successful." This hospital should be concerned about their standing with God and not just in meeting their FTEs. Authentic success and productivity should be understood better by this institution. Sharing of staff between units is a ridiculous way to cut cost and proves that our institution does not value people but instead just sees us as bodies. I know that much of the blame of all this is being placed on my immediate boss. This is not characteristic of great leadership. In the game of basketball, if a certain player is slow on transition and one of her teammates ends up fouling the shooter at the other end of the court, a great coach will not punish the girl who caused the foul. The blame is on the girl who was slow on transition and was not performing at her best for her team, and this action is what needs to be acknowledged as the problem. The foul is a secondary response to the real problem, and the response of a teammate's poor performance, in the back court, is what needs attention. It is important to search for the root of the problem when making a change. We hope to reach out to available nursing support systems in the community, across the state and throughout the country, to see what our options are and to also shed light on these important issues in the hope that we will be put in contact with godly leaders who value the importance and power of transformational leadership.

End of Letter

Chapter 17

Finding Purpose in the Moment

Every experience I encountered as a nurse and person I took care of had a different lesson to teach me. I did not want to think that they were just numbers or pawns. People meant something to me. I was built to be an advocate. God trained me through my years as a nurse to have hope when everything told me there was no hope. I let my patients tell me their story, and I listened, even when they had no voice. This part of my life was where I really found out what fortitude was. My early years in nursing was a time when I learned what having faith meant. I have stories that other people don't have. I have been through things others cannot even imagine, and this is how I grew to know God on an intimate level. At home I was struggling; at work there were more struggles, but God talked to me the whole time, and I listened. As a trauma nurse, I met a young man in his early twenties at a time in his life when he was active, on the move, and doing things. He was in his apartment on an ordinary day with his pregnant girlfriend when he got a phone call. The conversation led him outside, something about raining and his car windows were down, so he had better put them up. He was being set up but did not know this at the time. He did not realize someone was waiting for him outside. When he went outside, responding to the call, he was shot in the head. He did not die but was left in a coma, a vegetative state, and in a forever sleep on a ventilator. I was a young nurse and could not wrap my head around my position at his bedside, but I would learn many lessons from meeting him and lessons that would continue almost twenty years later.

During the beginning of his stay when his injury was still new, his pregnant girlfriend would come and visit, holding out hope for him to get better and to be the man she remembered before that fateful day when everything changed. After a while, she began to visit less, and then she never came back. I am sure it was hard for her to see him in that condition and not improving over so much time. His body changed. His muscles got weaker, and his arms and legs were lifeless and heavy. His hands and feet were turned in and stiff. He would never again be able to hold her hand. He went from holding her hand and being by her side to not even able to swallow his own spit. He could do nothing but lay in his prison without bars, held captive by his broken body, a shell of who he once was. He could not tell us if he was angry, hungry, sad, or happy. He had no preference for dinner. It was the same for him every night and administered by me, his nurse, through a tube in his stomach. He did not eat the same, look the same, or smell the same. Nothing about him remained except that inner being, which seemed distant, lost somewhere inside that broken body. He could not be reached through ways we normally communicated with people. Communication would be more mechanical, by touch and care, and you hoped he knew you were there even though he never showed signs of this knowledge. He was always in another world, a world that no one seemed to have access to. How do you find purpose in these moments? This was a sight I am sure was devastating to his family. You want to wake up and have it be a dream. This was the way it was so many times. People realized the reality of the situation and just stopped coming to see their loved one. People act in response to their senses. If they do not see a response to their efforts or a good feeling from their work, efforts, and affection, they just stop doing it. This is why we have so much divorce, foster kids, poor work ethic, depression, anxiety, obesity, and so forth. In this case, pain of what could be true, that their loved one will never recover or possibly will never even know they are there or be able to reciprocate their love and affection is too much for them. They will not get enough out of staying, so they leave. When people start to feel unimportant in a situation or like they deserve better than pain and sadness, or maybe they cannot cope, they leave. When they see no hope in the fight, they give up. They often cannot continue having hope that their love makes a difference when it is not rewarded and recognized. Sometimes no one sees our efforts but God alone, and this kind of love we show to others when there is nothing to gain for ourselves is unique and beautiful, rare. People often believe that love is only valuable if it can be reciprocated by the other party. Think of divorce and how many people leave because they just are not getting enough out of the marriage. I understand the leaving. I have my own times in life when I ask, "Is this worth it?" I understand the hurt and pain and the feeling of dread. In cases where I could not leave, because I refused to go, I learned to understand there had to be a reason for me to be there. I did this in my marriage, which I wanted to give up on so many times, and with my patients when reality told me there was nothing I could do, but God gave me hope. Sometimes I wanted to leave my marriage or leave nursing, but I chose to stay. I had to practice storge, which was the natural affection someone has for their family. If you learn to treat everyone you meet like family, you can love them even in desperate times. Sometimes you must leave a situation, but sometimes the right thing is to stay. I found that I needed to stay. There was a reason, a goal to be reached. It would take so much of my effort that God had to pull through because, humanly speaking, I was not enough on my own. I took care of this patient on many occasions and would come into his room, wondering what I could do for him, and asked myself why I was involved in this man's life. I had to do whatever I could do to take good care of him. I prayed for him and his girlfriend and unborn baby. I just looked at him, feeling so sad that he would never see his baby being born and that his child would never know their dad. He just lay there, seemingly unaware of the lives around him. He had no control of his body and did not consciously respond to outside stimulus. His movements were unintentional and reflexive. I would wash him up and turn him and get the pressure off his heels. I would wipe his drool and suction his airway as he coughed uncontrollably. I would pray for him to be healed. I changed his sheets and crushed his endless list of meds to put in his feeding tube to keep him alive for another day. I served him dinner through his feeding tube, knowing he could no longer have pizza night or Taco Tuesday or enjoy wing night with his friends. Where were his friends now? I thought. We were his friends now, the nurses. I wished him out of that bed and out of that life, but God had a plan, and I could not understand, but I loved that young man the best I could from my angle at the bedside.

At the time, my husband was escaping his life at home. He would sneak away whenever he could to get some time for himself and did not indulge in our kids' activities. I longed for him to be around and to appreciate the family God gave him, but he was always searching for something else. I knew what my husband had was precious, but he did not see it. I looked at this man in a coma with no chance to be a dad, and God was kneading me again, like dough, pressure on. I was learning to appreciate life. To even walk out of the hospital was a treat. If it was raining, to feel the rain on my body was a treat because this man could never feel the rain. To be cold from the snow was to experience something this man would never again see or enjoy or be bothered by. I appreciated my old house that I drove home to. I appreciated my body that was sore from those hard sixteen-hour shifts, but I could walk myself to the bath and sit in the hot water and soothe myself. I could hold my babies and look into their faces and watch them grow. I could cry if I wanted to, and many nights, I did, thinking about these patients who could no longer communicate with the outside world and how spoiled I was for being able to. This man could not cry or take a hot bath or even tell me that he wished he could. My life was changing, and I was being molded. This did not happen all at once, but over time, as I looked back at my experience with this patient and others like him, I learned more and more. I was thankful for the simplest things in life, never needing much of anything because worldly possessions are worthless. What could they do for this man? I went home for the night and continued to live life, but these patients seemed to just remain. They were found in their same bed, in their same room when I got back to work for each shift until they were stable enough to go back to their long-term recovery centers or otherwise. I began to pray for my husband to see and have vision as I was learning to see, and I began to embrace my duties and opportunities to love as a nurse. I could not believe in my heart this man was suffering in his state or that any of these patients were. I had to believe that we see these people suffering in this state, but I believe God holds them in a way we cannot see from the outside. He takes care of them and leaves them this way to help others to see him through the situation. All the while, he is preserving them and protecting them on the inside. These people are like geodes. They may appear damaged, banged up, and dusty on the outside; but on the inside, they are full of beauty, and that is where God is, preserving them, building them on the inside until they pass on. He still works on them. He always has a plan, and this is what I believe. These experiences are for others too, the people on the outside, to learn things and to grow close to God. People like me, the nurse. I prayed for that whole family as they came to my mind over the years. I decided to appreciate the lessons I learned from this man's story because through his story, the change in me could bring glory to God. When he meets Jesus, he could meet with good work under his belt. The work of teaching me about God's grace, mercy, love, and protection. As he fought in the bed, I fought from the bedside. He taught me storge and perseverance and how to pray for my family and continue to care about people when there seems to be no hope. God used this man to teach me and to now teach everyone who reads this story and chooses to gain perspective and to change. I believe this gives the young man power from his position in the bed. It gives him a voice. I am his nurse, so I need to be his voice, even today, maybe fifteen or so years later. I helped release that power for him in my willingness not to leave but, instead, to fight with him and for him, and this was through the power of God. That unborn baby would be about fifteen years old now, and I wonder how he or she is doing. Those encounters I had all those years ago did affect me. I keep these families in my heart, and even though I never knew whatever happened to that young man after he was transferred out, I know God loved him and took care of him because the God I know never lets us fight battles alone. This teaches us to help others fight their battles too even if they are fighting in a bed and they seem to have no voice or even when there seems to be no hope in the fight.

How much faith do you have? How tough are you that you can battle with someone and for someone when there seems to be no hope in the fight? I have been there. It is tough. But it is only a test. The reality is that God has it all under control. He just uses these situations to build us as we are all in his family, safe, well protected, strong, fierce, and beautiful. Count your blessings and do not fail the test.

Chapter 18

The Day I Was Interrogated on the Job

On September 28, shortly after 2:00 p.m., I was met in the hallway by one of my leaders who asked me to come meet with a human resource representative because she wanted to ask me some questions about my letter. It was important to meet soon to solve our unit's problems of many years, and I was willing, even though I was put on the spot, because God's Word tells us that we are always ready to speak truth as his Holy Spirit guides us. I had peace about telling the truth. I offered to stay at the hospital until 7:00 p.m. that day and work a twelve-hour shift since we were shorthanded. At this point, shortly after 2:00 p.m., I would normally be planning and preparing to start rounds for the last four hours of my shift. The two leaders and I were in the hallway, and one offered to take my work phone and cover my assignment while I left the floor to answer these questions. I agreed to go, as I was told this would only take a few minutes, though I didn't trust them, but I knew whatever I walked into, God was with me. I had to be a voice for my patients and for the other nurses, no matter the cost. I walked into the office and met the human resources rep. This was not the same human resources rep who was in the meeting the day before. It was just her and me in a small office. She told me she normally worked remotely but came in specifically to meet with me in person, so I would feel like my needs were being addressed. I have said before that I am interested in actions, not words, or in this case, stage setting. I continued to listen, but after she continued to say this was an "investigation" and that what was said in that room that day should not be discussed outside of that room and I was to keep the information "confidential," I did not trust her. I began wondering what this was. She told me that I could trust her and that we were alone, just me and her, so I could speak freely. This statement was also concerning because I speak freely and truthfully whether I am alone or in an audience of people, and this supports integrity. What was she implying? She asked me very detailed questions about my first letter and was asking me to interpret things I said in the letter. Why does my letter need to be interpreted? I was very careful to write in ways that people could understand. I was confused because all of what she asked me was very detailed in my letter. Why the need for this meeting? Was the plan to somehow entrap me? This began to feel like an interrogation and a scare tactic. It was mental jujitsu, but I don't play those simple mind games and don't get intimidated by simplemindedness, so I hoped she wasn't trying to waste my time. She kept saying we had a lot to cover and that she had a lot of questions for me and that my letter was very long, which she said repeatedly in that meeting. As time went on, I was beginning to wonder when this would end. Was she trying to make me believe this was punishment for speaking up? I am proud to speak truth and answer questions but not for the sake of being mocked. I prayed that my mind would be clear and that God would bring back all my memory of events and details so I could remain honest and a good witness of him. I needed to answer her questions, but the longer this went on, I was getting mentally tired. She began asking me to give her names of people, and this was not relevant, but I knew my coworkers did want change and had been willing to talk, but still, it was a way to build some kind of case, and I knew these kinds of companies never want to admit fault. They like to deny, delay, and deflect; and they had no case or right to waste more time fixing these issues. I had already worked eight hours that day on the floor. I had eight patients and had admitted a new C-section who I knew needed to get out of bed soon since she and I discussed a plan of care when she was admitted to the room on mom and baby, and she was motivated to ambulate as soon as she was allowed. There was no clock in this meeting room, so I did not know what time it was. I remembered I had taken a call from a doctor while in my patient's room, right before leaving my unit for this meeting but did not get a chance to put his order in the computer before leaving the floor, since I was caught in the hallway by the leaders. I thought this would only take a few minutes, like I was told, but now it seemed some time had passed, and the questions just kept coming. I was beginning to get nervous about all the work backing up for me and the fact that this order I took from the doctor was not documented. I wanted to be responsible for myself but remembered that my boss said she would cover my assignment, and I trusted God, so I continued answering questions. She continued with questions and addressed my statements about nurses in America having depression and higher suicide rates than other careers. She told me that therapy was available for nurses, meaning, to me, that the money-driven pressures would not stop, but we could get therapy to help cope with the abuse. I did tell her that I wanted support for my coworkers, but I meant support in making changes and getting to the root of the problems to stop the poor treatment of our staff and substandard care of patients, not put a Band-Aid on it. Even as I sat in that chair, the abuse of nurses continued. At first, I thought this program suggested would be good for the nurses, but I realized this was just a cover-up, an empty charity to gain our trust as we continued to be treated badly. Finally, I felt mentally drained. I told her this was a lot, and I could not remember the details of what she was asking me. My mind felt foggy. I had referred to my letter as my "first letter." She asked, "You mean there is another letter?" I told her I had a second letter, the one I was not allowed to read in the meeting. Then she said she would have to address that after she got back from vacation. Another familiar statement to me. It seems self is widely worshipped in leadership, and teamwork is only expected of the floor nurses. *Is everyone on vacation?* I thought. This is evidenced by her asking me in the beginning of the meeting what I meant in my letter when I said the environment for nurses on mom and baby and labor and delivery was toxic, even though I gave many examples and was very clear and detailed about why the environment was toxic. Then by her making me explain myself further and then by offering me therapy, it was as if she was attempting to devalue my concerns and assessments and then disrespecting me further by letting me know she was going on vacation but would make sure she connected again with me when she got back. She smiled and said that these requests I had would take time, which was a statement commonly used throughout leadership. "Delay, deny, deflect." This is more fitting for a mission statement for the organization than to say they serve Jesus. When she tried to justify her plan of stalling on fixing these problems, I responded by saying that not all these changes take time. I wanted her to know that I knew her game. I was familiar with the approach of impostor leadership, which is to "delay, deny, deflect." This is a common approach used by other agencies to save and make money by poor treatment of others. These tactics that were used by the leaders in this facility to escape accountability are not new, and I have seen this strategy used in many different facets. It is a low and dishonorable tactic. I was not new to this game as she may have thought. I have encountered this kind of battle plan before in places like insurance companies or banks that add unrealistic deadlines or small print to entrap clients. I've been through many situations, and I do understand these organizations have no idea who I am until I let them know who I am.

I decided to elaborate for a moment and do the work for her and give yet another example of the toxic environment that had developed. I said that when patients come to our unit and orders are not carried out from labor and delivery, it takes extra time for nurses to get these orders done and puts the patients in unsafe conditions. I was specifically thinking and then began elaborating on a time recently when a patient had a hemoglobin of 5.2, which is a dangerously low blood count, and there was an order to transfuse packed red blood cells in labor and delivery, but that order was never carried out until after the patient was transferred to mom and baby, delaying care for hours. These delays are often caused by young nurses who are training other young nurses to rush the transfer of patients, pushing the work off even when it is unsafe practice. This training is substandard and dangerous, but more importantly, it is unethical. These patients and nurses don't have time to wait for leaders to get back from their vacations to deal with these issues. If the leaders in labor and delivery checked the charts before patients came to mom and baby to make sure all the work was done, and understood the workload better and was willing to provide for the change, this problem would go away. Blaming young, inexperienced nurses is shameful, but this activity is tolerated by the leaders. Having a poor work ethic is encouraged in our country, but in health care it could mean the difference between life and death. This was a simple example of me interpreting my letter while using deductive and inductive reasoning. This would be, of course, if those in leadership understood the job of a nurse and were sold on the importance of carrying out all current duties and established treatment plans while the patient was in their care, stabilizing patients before transferring the patient to another unit. This would be to honor basic foundational principles and ethics in medicine. Deductive and inductive reasoning rely on logic, which allows one to travel from specific observations to broad generalizations. This was how I responded to her claim that change takes time. She told me if I had said it in that way from the beginning, it would have been understood better by leadership.

So I guess since they cannot blame time or young nurses, they will just claim I need therapy or that I did not explain the problems and solutions well enough for them to understand. More deflection. Was my very lengthy letter not long enough? Does it make me a bad communicator if the one I am talking to chooses not to listen and understand or is not capable of using logic? What I then realized in that "interrogation" was that these leaders must be incapable of reasoning in their own minds and I am expected to do this for them. I really thought I was addressing people with college degrees and experience in running organizations and professionals who understood the clinical properties and responsibilities in nursing. This type of execution by leaders could have started months ago and should have already been in use for years. There are many more of these very specific points that have gotten little to no attention, partially because the readers of the letters cannot reason in relation to the subject matter and partially because they are engulfed in behavioralism, having management titles without understanding, and cannot detect their position or specific responsibility to the problems at hand that God himself calls them to respond to. The most important reason for all of this is that they don't have a heart that God is in charge of. They have knowledge but cannot acknowledge truth, making whatever they do know useless (2 Timothy 3:6–9). When God is the filter of your heart, he teaches you how to respond lovingly to others. He disciplines us into absolute purity. In Proverbs, he teaches that when we delight in the Lord, he gives us the desires of our hearts. The desires in this workplace were not to love and channel truth because they did not delight in serving him. This is the root of the problem.

I am convinced that this organization has been very busy promoting behavioralism all throughout the administration and across the board of leaders. This is why they must follow algorithms and cannot think for themselves. It is a form of mental abuse. I realize that I may not find anyone in leadership who can think for themselves and can interpret my simple, yet intellectual and God-inspired writings and advice. Wisdom is lacking in this facility from years of not living by faith in God on a day-to-day basis because people are put in positions who cannot thrive independently or as part of the team but do have other backgrounds that this organization's top leadership favors, like obeying worldly standards and ideas that make financial rewards for them, which is regarded as a higher priority than the welfare of the human element of this business. Recognizing only things such as college degrees, titles, or maybe experience in administration as qualifying someone for a position, births and then fosters toxic environments in medicine. Allowing for the advancement of an unproductive employee/person through promotion or even bringing someone new into a leadership position whose interpersonal skills and personal awareness are lacking, creating a negative culture over time, is only admired by the unscrupulous. This disregard for others and lack of human element negatively affect this organization. The employees who are not self-motivated to act with honor but who can display professionalism, if it means keeping their jobs, will act based on how they feel on any given day, making them unpredictable and inconsistent. Instead of recognizing this as a negative and teaching ways to change, this bad behavior is ignored, continuing the attack using mental and verbal jujitsu, and many are caving under the simple attack. Those who stall and are found resisting accountability and change on their own part as leaders are not demanding respect and accountability of their staff across the board. This activity is moving up and down the chain and is the spine of the company, with the staff who display good character and who act with heart being on the chopping block. This is adding to patient dissatisfaction and high turnover rates for nurses. Even though attempts are made to shine light on poor treatment of others, including patients and employees, by certain staff, the behavior continues. Empathy is lost when people choose not to love others and refuse to put themselves in others' shoes. By not using attributes of authentic leadership, which is to serve with a pure heart, arrogance and unmerited boldness thrive. Building this kind of infrastructure will lead to failure. The mind and body will always fail, but one with a good heart will triumph over evil. This is why the military will have testing for good character in ways of letting soldiers go without food and sleep for long periods of time. Once the body is depleted, the mind does not function well and is not reliable, and a person's true colors will shine through. This is when the decisions made by the soldier will come from the heart, and this is how the soldier's true character and the condition of their heart will be revealed. This is how they choose people for specific missions that require integrity and honor to complete. The military has their own attacks from the devil, and some people represented in the military do not have good hearts, but it is a good strategy, and I pray God washes out the impurity there and in the medical field.

Finally, after my answering several ridiculous questions, the meeting ended. She said, "Wow, it is five o'clock already."

Five o'clock? I thought. What! I was in there for three hours! *How am I going to get my work done by seven? My patients…they must be wondering where I am!"*

I rushed back to the unit and got my phone from the leader and hoped that she had things caught up for me. I sat down at the nurses' station and put the order from the doctor into the computer that I took right before getting called into that meeting. Just then, I noticed the call light was ringing. It was the husband from the room of my new C-section. The secretary answered the light, and I heard him speaking through the intercom. "Um, our nurse said she would be in here to get my wife up and out of bed at four o'clock, but that was an hour ago, and we still have not seen her," he said. I just began to feel hot. My neck was getting warm, and my throat began to feel tight, as I could hear her IV pump beeping in the background through the intercom. The leader took my phone but apparently did not do any required care. My meds needed to be given, babies assessments were late, and my new C-section was supposed to be ambulating…

    Nurses do not always even take their lunch breaks on my unit because their work will be waiting for them when they get back, and its either do not take lunch and leave on time or take lunch and leave late. We do not have relief nurses to take our phones and maintain the flow while we are off the floor. Many times, we get called from our patients, and our lunch is interrupted. We are discouraged by management to mention on the time clock that we did not get a lunch break, and we are also discouraged from staying over to finish our work if we must stay late because they don't want to pay overtime. This is why nurses do not always document that they did not take a lunch break. I just spent three hours in this room with no clock, being interrogated while my assessments, I and O's, meds, and eight-hour post-op care was just left behind. Work was building up while I was away and waiting for me when I got back. I was amazed that I lost such track of time in that little room. Apparently, my leader just thought there was no work needing to be done in those three hours. At 2:00 p.m. we start getting things ready for our next round. I went straight to the office for questioning at that time, and the leader took my phone and told me she was covering for me while I was off the unit, but nothing was done when I got back, and my call light was going off with my patients having no idea where I had been. I had never been in a situation like that before and vowed I would never again trust these people. I felt my face getting warm as I thought of all this and how fast I would have to work. I apologized to my C-section patient and her husband and told them I was called to a meeting, but that seemed like a lame excuse even though it was true. After I made rounds and finished my work the best I could and the next shift was coming on, I was overwhelmed and was quickly charting at the nurses' station as the leader again talked about birthdays, anniversaries, and whiteboards with her forced positive, bubbly attitude, and I just about melted in my body. I was sitting there in the chair charting, sweating, and had just been abused while my patients got no care. Does she even understand what just happened to me and my patients? Instead of taking care of my patients while I was being interrogated for three hours, she must have been looking up nurses' birthdays and checking whiteboards to make sure they were updated. *What difference does it make if the whiteboards are filled out if the work is not getting done and patients aren't even getting rounded on by the one telling us to make rounds? The focus is way off. This whole establishment is backwards*, I thought. This is the exact reason nurses are leaving the field. It encourages to not work with a good heart.

About two weeks later, October 14, it was about 3:00 p.m. when I got a call from the labor and delivery leadership that this same human resource representative was there and wanted to meet with me again. I told her absolutely not! The next thing I knew, a leader was there in the nurses' station with me and told me this woman was in a leader's office just a few feet away and just had a few questions for me. Now I was being harassed on the unit and followed around. Just a few questions, huh? This was what she said last time, and that was a three-hour situation. I would not go. My coworkers, including the two other members from the "task force" were there that day. I told the nurses this woman was back to ask me questions, and they told me not to go in alone. Absolutely not. "You are not going alone," they said. They were going to go with me, but then one of the nurses suggested to have the rep come out to the nurses' station, and we could all together as a group answer her questions since we all felt the same way. I and a coworker went into the office, and I told the rep I would answer her questions in the nurses' station with the other nurses, and she hesitated. She tried to encourage me to just stay in the office by saying it would not take long, and we were just recapping from the last meeting. I said no again, and she was reluctant but did finally agree to come to the nurses' station saying this did catch her off guard.

The nurses all gathered around and began speaking up and telling her all the same things I had wrote in my letters and had talked to her about in the meeting. They said they would not need therapy that was offered by the rep if the hospital did what was right and made appropriate changes. She offered to have someone come and shadow us nurses to see what our day was like. We said this was not necessary. A high-level leader also had made that suggestion earlier that day, and this is ridiculous. How can someone, who isn't even a nurse, shadow a nurse for a few hours and know what she really goes through? Is she going to take on a full assignment for twelve hours on a busy day and do this for weeks on end and go home to kids and a husband that need her while getting paid a wage that is not fair? No, she will not. This is arrogance speaking and would not be useful for her to shadow a nurse and then think she knows what a nurse at this hospital or any hospital goes through. It would just be something for her to write down in her work journal to say she tried to relate or assess the conditions, conditions she is getting paid to be aware of already, through discernment, empathy, engagement, reasoning, integrity, transparency, and all the other attributes of authentic leadership. The representative went on to say we needed to be positive instead of negative because both are contagious. Was she implying that we are negative for being honest? We were negative because we talked about the negative environment we worked in? We make the unit negative because we say the truth? I do believe this institution cannot handle the truth. They suppress it at all costs. They want to sit and talk about birthdays, vacations, homework, meetings, and shadowing instead of getting into the hard work and executing plans. If FTEs are creating a toxic environment for nurses and poor productivity by way of causing high turnover rates and dangerous patient experiences, then change the FTEs. Stop buying new businesses and fix the ones you are responsible for. Figure out why the formula is not producing a positive environment instead of pretending the environment is a positive one and trying to convince us that it is.

The rep chose to continue to mock me as she said that a better way of expression would have been, instead of writing my letter, to make a bullet-point spreadsheet for leadership so they could see exactly what we were saying needs to change. Once again, gaslighting was the game played here. I am not in any way interested in doing leadership's job or responding to narcissistic behavior, but I am hoping to inspire them to be responsible for the position they are in. Why should I think for these individuals when we would all benefit from them thinking for themselves while acknowledging truth? I gave them several examples of the toxic behavior and then spelled it out in person in the interrogation room, doing all the reasoning for them. Why do I need to now draw them pictures and diagrams of what I already wrote up in letters and was forced to explain in detail for three straight hours? Now I should go home and draw you a diagram? This is an example of delay. So now we've had meetings, interrogations, letters, explanations, phone calls, texts, more meetings, and now you want pictures, diagrams, and bullet-point spreadsheets. Delay, delay, delay. I will not be told by her or anyone else to believe this operation is healthy or motivated by positivity. I obey God's commands, and I am faithful to him and obedient to his call. I have even more perseverance than vacations they take, so I was not falling victim to these simple tactics. I acknowledge truth. God is my therapy.

She told us that she would go back and write up a bullet-point spreadsheet and present it to leadership herself. Finally, some good news. It had been over two months since my first meeting with leadership. I was thankful that someone finally was willing to lift a finger toward the betterment of the unit. (I never ended up seeing this drawn up, so I cannot say if she did it or not.) I wonder if this is considered by the top executives in this institution to be good productivity. Were they suggesting that after two months and eight leadership representatives, a bullet-point spreadsheet with the selling points of change, which were spelled out in detail from none other than the humble floor nurses, was worth all the leadership wages represented? I am pretty sure one of my middle school kids could have drawn up that spreadsheet easily after all the info was provided, and they would do it without mocking those who provided the information. The rep told me several times that I caught her off guard by asking her to meet in front of all the nurses and not just me. I knew leadership would try to single me out, and it would be easier to prove one person wrong instead of a group or better yet the whole unit. I proved to be someone who didn't back down, and they could not prove what I said wrong because it was truth, and this seemed to upset them. She also said she was trying to keep her voice down so the patients did not hear what we were talking about. When truth is desired and transparency respected, there is no need to keep quiet. Patients are experiencing the effects of the mismanagement. Was she implying that it is okay, that they are not getting the best care, if they do not know about it? Do they think they are cared about because someone rounds on them and asks if the nurse came in the room in the last hour? Did she think I was lying when I said I was not acting alone but that these views were held by many nurses on our unit? She must not have believed me, or she would not have been caught off guard when everyone wanted to speak up. She should not be worried about what the patients hear if they are hearing the truth, and if the truth is being lived out at this facility and something to be proud of, then why keep quiet? After forty minutes of my coworkers being able to speak up, the nurses told the rep that they did not even want to bring these matters up anymore because it had been years of us talking and no one listening. We were then told by her to be positive and not negative.

    Again, gaslighting. We are mocked every day in this institution, and my prayer is that as truth has been made known, leadership will desire to follow God's command to love others and to do what is right in seeing us as valuable and worth changing for. If we all focused on living our lives as an obedient service involving body, mind, and spirit as a form of worship, and this life we live reflected a specific daily process and not just ritualistic activity in the hospital, things would change. This establishment has decided what is considered good, bad, and productive, which leads to a perversion of the core, a false reality, and a spawning of ideas with no cohesiveness to be considered and tried out. I have continued in my work to promote and facilitate faith and grace. By encouraging my coworkers and supporting them as they think of themselves in sober judgment, denouncing false modesty on their journey to make a change, they are living out Romans 12:3, acting as conduits for faith and grace to move through us, as they are given to us by God. This is what we have hope in, and this is where the power of God resides. This is what fuels our fire and is how we can continue to serve daily, while hoping and praying for change.

On Friday, October 21, the human resource rep was back and was questioning the nurses once again. I said I was not going in the office because I had nothing more to talk about, and I did not want to get stuck in there again like I had before. I was asked by the charge nurse to go in to let her know that there was no one left to question. I told the rep this, and she asked me to answer some more questions for her. I said no, that I had nothing more to say, but she insisted. I reluctantly sat down, realizing I was going against myself, and now I was just being harassed in the workplace. This time I was more aware of who she was, so I would not stay in there for more than a couple questions. She told me this was to be confidential and not to be talked about outside of the office to my coworkers so everyone can have a fresh perspective. Then she asked me if I got to take my breaks and lunches. I wondered why this could not be discussed with my coworkers because we all talk about this and everything else I wrote about and have talked about for years. I told her I take my lunch breaks sometimes. She asked what I meant. I said, "Sometimes I do, and sometimes I do not." This questioning is ridiculous because it is well-known that we do not get to take our breaks all the time because we run understaffed. In fact, the hospital saves money canceling nurses all the time but requires them to be on call all day until their shift is over without being compensated for their on-call time. I am tired of being questioned on these issues. I am glad my coworkers are taking advantage of the opportunity to speak up, but I have been questioned repeatedly on these issues. When is enough, enough? I only answered a couple questions and then left the room. A senior leader was again on the unit that day, talking to the nurses in the nurses' station about shadowing. Not only will this not be useful, but how many times is she going to bring this up before either doing it or moving on to another idea? This is just another stall. She should already know what is happening on this unit, if not on her own, by way of my very detailed writings and all the nurses speaking up. Nurses have thanked me and told me they were glad I was doing this, speaking out in truth for change, because they did not have the energy or a way with words or just that they were afraid of the backlash. A nurse recently told me she was proud of what I was doing, but she was afraid for me and did not want to be seen talking to me about any of this because she feared for her own job. I have a greater respect for God than a fear of this world. The Bible teaches me that God's power defies the world's principles when you are obedient and acting in faith. Just like when Peter walked on the water. Gravity says that he should have sunk, but because God's grace was sufficient, and through faith and God's grace, power was released, and Peter did not sink. It was only when he took his eyes off Jesus and saw the wind and waves that he then began to sink; even still Jesus saved him. He quickly shifted from the spiritual action to the corporeal action. Once he focused on fear and the laws of gravity, he sank. I understand through faith that God is protecting me in this, and there is power in that. It is through God's authority that I speak, and he is sovereign. It is time that this organization, and the nursing field in general, stop suppressing nurses but, instead, support them and let them work through their gifts. There is power in this, and holding back on this to maintain excessive control is an attack on God.

Chapter 19

The Drug Search and Nurses Questioned

These letters were further submitted in October 2022. Thinking back at the process thus far, I could see what was happening, and it happens all the time and in all our lives, but we live such busy lives, and we often do not pay attention to this realization. I was powerful, and I was being built. I had faith that things were happening even though I didn't see it all happening right then. After these letters went out, a senior leader of the hospital had visited the unit and finally decided to put scrubs on and made rounds on the unit, following a nurse for the day. The idea was that she could maybe see what the nurses found to be so difficult and what can be done to change. Ultimately, it was a form of micromanaging, and it was an action that proved she did not value nurse's opinions and information provided. She had to prove us wrong. The same day she showed up to work alongside a nurse, there was word that someone smelled marijuana in a hallway near the nurses' locker room. This area is very close to the waiting room, and the smell of marijuana is a common occurrence on our unit. It has always been that way since I started on that unit fourteen years ago. I believe it is maybe due to the age of our patients and the area we serve. We never allowed smoking on the unit, but people would come in after smoking and would smell up the unit. The nurses are used to it. This day, however, when a senior leader was shadowing, the police were called and the drug dogs brought in. The nurses' lockers and the break room were searched. This was something I had never heard ever being done in my almost twenty years of working for this facility. Why search the nurses' lockers? Was this another scare tactic? Another try at incriminating the nurses or smearing their names so no one would believe our stories? After the search, a nurse found her coworker's purse in her locker, and their belongings were tossed about. The nurses were not aware of the search at the time and were not there while their things were gone through. How was this legal? The police found some pills and syringes in the locker of a nurse who was questioned about these items. Things like Motrin and Colace were the medicines found, which were normal everyday mild over-the-counter meds we would give to patients, not something a nurse would be stealing or abusing, but they still made the nurse explain as if she was in trouble for something. This seemed like another form of harassment and punishment for us speaking up. Sometimes as the days are long and we are always shorthanded, the nurses would put the packaged pills or unused extra syringes in their pocket if the patient did not want them when the nurse made rounds, and then eventually, when she had time, the nurse would put them in the "return to pharmacy bin" or supply drawer in the med room. The nurse questioned explained that sometimes she was so busy that she did not get a chance to do this, allowing the meds to accrue in her locker until a day came when she would collect the stack and drop them in the bin. What nurse does not use syringes in her everyday life at work? It appeared that this was a tactic to investigate the nurses and to find fault in them since we were demanding change and better treatment. It seemed they were displaced from the everyday reality of a nurse's life. To my understanding, the senior leader who suggested shadowing was not a nurse. To make it appear that you can pull up your hair and show up to the unit in scrubs and follow a nurse around and believe you understand their position and what any of them went through on the daily was proof of the arrogance represented in leadership there. To search the nurses' lockers during the workday without their knowledge and let them find their personal property such as their wallet, credit cards, and purse rummaged through and then carelessly thrown into someone else's locker is unethical, immoral, and unjustified behavior.

    They continued to investigate to seemingly try to find ways to smear the nurses' reputations so that their views or values would not be validated. They sent people from human resources to the unit on certain shifts to be a "listening ear." They would bring "homemade cookies" and come onto the unit at the end of our shift to tell us that if we wanted, we could come talk to them privately in a back room to discuss our feelings and concerns since they heard in the letter that "nurses go home and do things." They were using the information from my letter against us to mock us and make us seem like the problem. I spoke about how nurses drink alcohol, cry, battle depression and anxiety at times, and that nurses have high suicide rates in America. They saw this and tried to make us believe we had problems and needed to be saved, and we needed their help. We were not buying it. They wanted to prove by our speaking truth that we were people who had problems and that our testimonies of what we observed on the unit was a figment of our imagination and the real problem was with us, as if we just had trouble dealing with life and this is why we saw our unit as a toxic environment. They were gaslighting us, and we knew it. We were smart, and we were confident in who we were. We knew we had value. We knew we were dealing with sin disguising itself as narcissism. They wanted us to believe we were troubled people who needed cookies and therapy. I believe no one went to eat those cookies or talked to those people who were thought to try to use our words against us. How convenient for their fight against us if they would have found illegal drugs in our lockers, which they didn't. How convenient would it have been if we trusted them with our "feelings" so they could incriminate us in the records they kept. They couldn't. They had no idea who they were dealing with. Evil never triumphs over good, and we knew they were wrong in their actions toward us. All their lame and petty attempts to scare us into keeping quiet did not work.

Chapter 20

Another Letter and the Meeting with Corporate

It was Thursday, December 22, 2022, when I was called to yet another meeting by the labor and delivery leadership. I was once again on the unit with an assignment and hesitant to go, but this would be a meeting with corporate representatives and through a zoom call. This was another letter I wrote that I was called there to discuss. This would be my third letter. This time the letter was in response to a physician who decided he had the right to harass and mistreat the nurses on the unit. He thought this because as I mentioned before, the nurses were not protected by leadership from the unmerited pride of the doctors. They knew they could get away with abusing staff because the leaders did; it was the culture there. I decided this was where it should stop.

Dear leadership,

On November 13, 2022, I worked an on-call shift from 7:00 a.m. to 11:30 a.m. That morning, nurses were texted early before coming in and asked if they would be willing to take extra patients so a night-shift nurse would not get mandated to stay over. Once again, our facility was robbing Peter to pay Paul. The night before, a night-shift nurse worked a twelve-hour shift and was mandated over to day turn. A nurse relieved her, and she still then had an hour drive home. We were all tired that morning, and some of us had been there the day before, working hard. We were there in good spirits, ready to take on the day, smiling and leaning on each other and sharing in each other's fortitude. Suddenly, the morale had changed as we were greeted by a doctor, known to be in leadership. I was walking past the nurses' station when I heard him talking, and I knew what he was up to. His tone and content of conversation gave him away as I remembered, I had a familiar conversation with him in this same nurses' station a few months before. He was telling us that we, mom and baby nurses, were the reason that discharges did not get out fast enough and that we caused a kink in the flow of the unit and process of discharge. I explained to him that we were the end of the hospital stay, and the problems began from the beginning when the patients were admitted, and many things along the way caused kinks. I explained these problems in detail through the letters I submitted to this hospital, corporate, and the state. He continued to argue in our conversation that we did not work fast enough and were not efficient. He asked questions that proved he did not know our job or understood what was expected of us, so I made it easy for him and explained, "You don't know what you don't know." I recognized his trying to rationalize a situation he had no idea about and was just randomly placing blame because he would not do what it took to acknowledge the truth. He turned and left the unit after my statement, and the heated event was neutralized by truth.

THE VOICE OF TRUTH

This day, November 13, when I was walking past the nurses' station and I recognized his tone, I decided to let him talk to see if since the last experience of mocking the nurses in the nurses' station he had learned anything. He raised his voice to get the nurse's attention. He said that if circumcisions are not done by the day of discharge, it is the nurse's fault because she should be more forceful, pushing the issues and telling the doctors the circs need to be done. He asked, "How are the doctors supposed to know that circs need to be done if the nurses do not tell them?" He then said that nurses need to prioritize better. The charge nurse said she had eight patients, and he said, "So you mean four patients," implying that babies do not count as patients. The nurses told him the babies are a lot of work, and he mocked us by sarcastically saying that he has double the patients then, implying that babies take no work and we take credit for doing nothing. He said that our discharges had better be out by 11:00, and he'd better not see any of us sitting around. After threatening us, he informed us that labor and delivery was backed up with several postpartum patients, and we needed to clear our patients out so we can move those patients over. He said that they are not going to pay millions of dollars to expand our unit, so it's our job to improvise. He said that labor and delivery nurses have some things to say about us too but that he was not going to stir the pot. After he finished dehumanizing the nurses with his ridiculous lecture, he told the nurses to look how long they had been sitting there (listening to him) and that they needed to get to work. We did not see him for a little while and heard that he went over to labor and delivery and reportedly said that he had to hide over there because he just pissed off the mom and baby nurses. After he left, the charge nurse who had over thirty years of experience was obviously overwhelmed by the harassment and abuse from the doctor. She was choked up, began to cry, and said she just couldn't take it there and couldn't believe how he treated us. I told her the truth that she was okay and that his response had no merit. He did not determine her worth, and his maleficent ideologies should be paid no mind. Other nurses said they felt like they did a bad job after hearing him talk, but I told them this is not true. Another nurse just shook her head, disappointed at his ridiculous, unprofessional behavior. I was not shocked and was not moved by his disrespectful and immature behavior because he had done it before, and his responses have no foundation of truth, but this was out of line and unacceptable and on a larger scale than I have seen before, and the situation was able to escalate this time because his prior behavior was not dealt with, and he chose not to learn. A short time had passed since his lecture, and he returned to the unit and harassed nurses further about their patients, asking why they were not discharged yet, attempting to disregard and devalue the scrupulous intentions of the nurses who discharge patients with care. One nurse told him that her patient had been nauseated, taking Zofran, and not able to take oral pills yet. He said to discharge her anyway, suggesting that the nurse's evaluation and assessment of the patient did not matter and was not validated. The nurse was uncomfortable with discharging this patient, and the patient went home in a wheelchair with an emesis basin.

Patients were telling the nurses they knew we were in a bed crunch and knew we needed their bed, so they would have to leave. Why would human resources work to keep conversations about these things quiet from the patients in the past, but now the patients are made to feel like they are obligated to leave before they are ready because of the condition of the hospital? Who was telling these patients we were in a bed crunch and they needed to leave? This should not be their concern. The nurses were impressed that the patients knew of the trouble the hospital was in. The patients deserve to feel safe and welcomed. It is a double standard to preach good health but to not support it, and now the patients are hearing the truth about the health care system and how their first goal it to be "productive" on paper and in dollar signs. It is spreading knowledge of the disrespect these women and babies are receiving from our leaders, and we do not want to be part of that. The nurses do not support this, and neither do many doctors who have chosen to leave the traditional system to have time to spend with patients.

One nurse was called out of her patient's room by the doctor who asked her why the patient was not gone yet when she and the baby had discharge orders. He did not understand the discharge process and apparently did not realize a baby must stay for two hours after a circumcision is completed to be evaluated for bleeding. This was the protocol. He was further distracting nurses and putting patient safety in jeopardy by trying to rush them out before they were ready and all care was completed, encouraging the breach of policy and procedure. The nurses were frustrated by being forced to rush the process of discharge regardless of the individual needs of the patients and the expected role of the nurses. The doctor caught one nurse in the hallway and asked her what she was doing. "Going to lunch?" he asked, implying this would be unacceptable. She told him no, she was not going to lunch; she was walking to the other unit because she had a patient over there. Having patients on two different units is frowned upon by the American Nurses Association, but still our leadership supports this on a regular basis. Nurses had nine patients a piece that day, well over the suggested patient load as recognized by the nursing standards. People were not taking breaks, and he was rubbing it in and mocking us by his unmerited actions toward us and the patients. I was not approached by the doctor this day even though I had two sets of discharges. He also did not circumcise the baby I was taking care of who was a clinic patient, even though he was rounding for the clinic that day and even though one of the topics discussed was how circumcisions are not done in a timely manner by the doctors and are put off until discharge day, causing a kink in the system. Was he trying to implicate himself, or was this God unveiling more truth in the situation? Why didn't he thank me for coming in extra to help the unit function better that day instead of just complaining and pushing blame? I support the entire group of nurses who were there that day, and I stand behind them. I am their advocate, and I do believe this is why this doctor did not approach me this day even though

I had two sets of discharges. He did not question me because he knows that I know the truth. He knows I do not support or tolerate dehumanization and harassment in the workplace. He knows I support integrity, honor, compassion, and efficiency. If he is looking to place blame, he is looking in the wrong place, and he knows that I know this. Every single nurse on the floor that day works hard and does their job well, and I can attest to this. I am impressed with them as nurses. Some are mothers and wives as well, multitasking in several roles, and they are all women made in God's image. They deserve respect, and I will always push and fight for this on my unit and in every aspect of my life. They are someone's daughter, someone's mother, someone's sister, and friend. They should be honored by this doctor and this organization, respected as people of importance and value. As a man, this doctor should take his role seriously. Woman were made to be a man's help. This is scriptural. We respect this. We understand this. We respect the doctors, whether man or woman, but as a man, does he understand his role concerning the woman? He should protect her, respect her, and regard her as his equal. She came from him. Bone of his bone, flesh of his flesh (Genesis 2:23). God formed woman from man, and men are born of women so that all things are of God (1 Corinthians 11:12). Does the doctor believe this? As part of this "ministry" that claims to serve Jesus, why would he be appointed as a leader if he does not believe this? If he believed this, wouldn't it show in his actions, since whatever is in the heart overflows in one's actions? He has much potential, and the sky is the limit if he would just recognize his worth and purpose in his position. Why did our leadership not address this issue with us and call a meeting to discuss this? Does our boss support this behavior? Does she not support the very people she represents? Is she even qualified to distinguish wrong in this situation or is she just practicing religious activity on the unit? Does she know her worth? These are big questions, and who can answer them? They are rhetorical questions because the truth is in plain sight to those who obey God and seek him, and this is what is lacking on our unit and in our facility (Revelation 2:17).

    I was informed that, apparently, this doctor, a man in leadership at this facility, went to leadership that week and said that nurses were not nice to him and did not respond appropriately to his display of character that day after they told him they disagreed with him, and they took offense to his attitude and actions that day. So another leadership representative was made aware (from his side of the story) of what happened that day. He tried to put up a smoke screen and make the nurses the scapegoat for his arrogance, disregard for patients, and lack of dignity and decency in response to nurses, as well as this facility's lack of efficient operation secondary to a lack of space and workers to serve many patients. His actions show disrespect and ignorance of the basic unbending principles of the one who made us all and allowed us to be put in these positions in the first place, through grace. I do not support this, and this is the very thing stirring up dissension between the units and is also negatively contributing to and impacting the already unsafe and unhealthy environment we have in the mom and baby and labor and delivery units. On a larger and much more important scale, this type of activity does not serve God. You cannot serve two masters. You can either serve God or serve the devil, and there is no place in between. God says choose this day who you will serve. You cannot rebuke if you do not first teach, and you cannot teach if you have no knowledge, wisdom, or understanding of the subject. The honor of rebuking goes to those who teach what they have learned, and if you have not learned, you cannot teach. This facility is acting in and respecting dishonor by allowing this to continue.

This doctor continues to come to the unit, rushing patients out even when they are uncomfortable and unsettled about leaving, and nurses are being forced to comply. Rights of mothers and babies in the community are not protected by this kind of activity. Mothers and infants are in a vulnerable state in the postpartum period. This time is critical to address their needs during recovery and to ensure their health of mind, body, and spirit and will impact the mother and child over the first entire year following delivery but also will follow them and can drastically affect them throughout their whole life. This is recognized by Health and Human Services and makes an impact on the community and the country. These days given to them in the postpartum period to recover in the hospital through their insurance is a right we are stripping them of by sending them home early like we are a baby mill and they are just objects on a conveyor belt.

As organizations still fight to address the concern of the maternal health crisis in the United States by way of policies and programs,

I see something that apparently is not being addressed. I do hope to assist CMS as they request information and are seeking information to assist in understanding and uncovering the problems concerning this health crisis in the United Sates. Arrogance plays a big role in the problem, and people in leadership contribute to the negative by refusing to work as a team and recognize that we have a moral obligation to these patients to send them home rested and in good health in order to give them the best chance at a healthy foundation going forward after delivery. If a patient is not ambulating well, taking in proper nutrients yet, or their baby perhaps has not established an acceptable eating routine, this calls for concern and should not be overlooked. Patients should not be sent home just because we do not have beds for them. Policy development is useless if those who implement the policy have no honor. This is where the problem lies. Even if you implement all recommended interventions and report that you are participating in quality collaborative measures, you are fooling yourself to believe you are justified while problems continue right under your noses. Jesus took religion to the cross when he died for us. Religious acts of only checking boxes and crossing t's and dotting i's will not count for anything on judgment day. None of that show of worldly competency will save us. God teaches us this in his word, and this teaching needs to be the basis for how we live and treat each other in the workplace, especially patients. This principle comes first before any policy or procedure. Aristotle said, "Educating the mind without educating the heart is no education at all." Years and years of simply going through the motions has dulled the spiritual senses of this organization's leadership, and this has gotten us to even lower levels of disrespect, stemming from the continuation of seeing objects, dollar signs, and deadlines instead of people, passion, and purpose. I hope to contribute to the gathering of data/information as CMS is expanding its efforts to better understand important influencers of health and to target specific points that improve quality of care and to identify imbalances in outcomes. If they are really working to bridge gaps in best practice, they will need to know that people who cannot find within themselves the courage to fight for and preserve what is right, which begins with God and his natural law, they will never deliver quality health care to anyone. It just cannot be done, and this crisis in our country will never change for the better, no matter how much data is collected, how many numbers are run, or how many programs are coordinated across. Without God, the veil remains and the mind is dull and hardened (2 Corinthians 3:14). I do hope this problem is addressed, repentance is practiced, and healing can begin.

End of letter

I agreed to go to the meeting with the corporate representatives that day to discuss this last letter I wrote but let leadership know of my apprehension to go alone. Thankfully, my friend, someone who was on the task force and a reliable support person, open-minded, confident, and honest, was willing to come with me to this meeting. Thank God for her and her continued love and support throughout the journey to expose truth. We arrived in the office, and there were two reps on the zoom call. They asked me some specific questions about the letter I submitted about the doctor and the situation involving the mistreatment of nurses that specific day. I was glad to answer questions. They were very professional. They asked me if other doctors were involved in this treatment of nurses. I explained that my concern was that this specific doctor's actions, if not corrected and addressed as unacceptable, would negatively influence other members of the team in leadership, including other doctors, to also engage in this behavior. They said they understood. He was only supporting the system. It was this very system they were trying to preserve by trying to isolate him alone as a problem. They had a way of doing this. Leadership would punish different people and pluck them out so it looked like they were taking a stand against evil. Meanwhile, they were just causing a distraction so they could continue to advance the dysfunctional system. This would be the "deflection" part of their "deny, deflect, delay" strategy. They just circled through this strategy, and I was able to witness this throughout my journey as an advocate for change. I explained that I was humbled to have sent the letter about the doctor and that we all make mistakes, but that patients' safety and nurses' good health were my main concerns. I had nothing against this doctor other than his support of a system that did not serve the public or him. The meeting went well and was relatively short and to the point. These were corporate reps. About a half hour later, leadership came to me again and asked me to meet on another zoom call with a rep from human resources. This time it was the woman I had met with who interrogated me for three hours a few months earlier and who I did not trust. I told her I would agree to meet, but I wanted to bring the same coworker with me who attended the corporate meeting with me. We walked into the meeting, and this atmosphere was not the same as the last meeting that day with the corporate reps. I sensed the disconnect immediately. I said hello and my coworker said hello. I introduced my coworker and said that I wanted her to be there as my witness during the meeting. The human resource rep, who had hesitated in the past when I wanted to speak with witnesses around, looked at me and said that was not acceptable. She said this was to be a private meeting with only her and me. I immediately knew this was not a safe meeting. There is a time to speak in private if both parties are in agreement, but I did not agree with meeting alone. I know that the devil loves to work on us when we are alone, just like he tempted Jesus in the desert. I told her that I was willing to answer any questions she had and I was willing to be transparent, honest, and forthright but that I was not willing to speak to her alone. The last meetings she had with me, the interrogation, the drug search, the free cookies in exchange for speaking were all catching up to me. I was not willing to play along. She said that she was going to put down that I was refusing to speak to her and have the meeting. I said that was a lie. I told her that I was very willing to speak to her but not without a witness. I said that what happened that day, the thing we were there to discuss, happened in public, so why did we need to meet privately about it? She could not answer me and would not let the meeting continue with my witness present. I told her to have a nice day, and she did not seem very happy with me. My coworker and I got up from our seats and left the room, and I later let corporate know through an email of the situation. I told corporate in the email the truth, that I was very willing to provide information but not alone. The corporate rep had told me in our meeting that she was a resource for me, and if I needed anything, to let her know, so I decided to include her in this. I did not hear back from her, though. The paper trail was made of my side of the story because I had no idea what the human resource rep put down as to why we did not have the meeting. When you speak the truth, it will put you in a position where you find yourself watching your back, and people will try to make you feel vulnerable. You will have a target on your back. This is why people do not stand up to these corporations and to everyday people in their lives including family, schools, coaches, parents, and so forth. They do not want the backlash. I say welcome it. The responsibility is there to be honest anyway, and God expects us to be involved, pushing toward the light. This means the battle is ours. We can choose to fight or just sit on our sword; the choice is ours. God is supreme. The only power people have is that which is given to them from God, just like what Jesus told Pilate when Pilate claimed he had the power to release Jesus. These people had no power over me. They could not take my job or punish me or anything else without God's approval, and I was following his lead, so I was in complete safety. They were not making enough change for the better in our facility. Units did not get separated. There was still no nursery nurse to do circs, blood work, and other tasks, and we were still working with seven or eight patients on most days. They did eventually hire an LPN for the nursery, which was a start, but she was per diem, and we needed a permanent nurse in there. I was canceled over and over again, which was them robbing Peter to pay Paul. They let the LPN be hired, but I was staying home. It was reported to me that on a day that I was made to stay home, my coworker had eight patients with one being in COVID isolation. Other nurses were reporting the days were very busy on days I was made to stay home. There were many days where nurses had six patient assignments, and some nurses did report that all the work we did in reporting the issues was paying off in some ways. We did see some positive change, and they reported they felt relieved as the assignments were more realistic at times. This was reassuring, but still I knew so much could get better. The pressures put on the nurses should be reduced. I wanted this for them.

Weak leaders make a choice to believe their hands are tied by upper management. While their hands are tied, they take vacations and are honored by the company for continuing to do a good job being controlled by them, people who are under the influence of the world. It is a form of slavery. They continue using words like *budget* and *FTEs* to keep playing the field and use these words to push blame on something else for the poor treatment of patients and nurses that they are responsible for. This is the "deflect" part of their game. We blame our kids for why our house is a mess or why we do not have money or sleep. We blame our jobs or inflation for why we do not have enough money to pay our bills. We blame our teachers for why we cannot learn the subject matter. We blame our parents for childhood trauma we experienced that we still cannot overcome as adults. We blame the government for why we decided to do something that was against our beliefs. We blame restaurants for making food that did not satisfy. We blame viruses for causing illness that we believe took people away from us and which continues to disrupt our lives and our comfort. While people are accountable for their disobedience to God in all these situations, these circumstances do not give power in causing any harm to us, unless we allow it. We must learn cause and effect from God's eyes. We must learn to understand our position of power that comes from being found in Christ and what this affords us on planet Earth. We also must understand that not all "good people" go to heaven. This is another distraction just to keep us comfortable in a world that is dark. If a company finds favor in you and gives you a certificate of achievement, you believe you have done good works even though these organizations are evil. If your parents, coaches, or spouses are proud of you, you believe you have done a good work. You believe if you won a trophy, you did something good. What does God say about you? Who are these people giving out awards influenced by? Maybe you did a good job. Maybe inflation is robbing you of money. Maybe you did work hard to get a trophy. I'm talking about taking the concept deeper. Heaven is a spiritual place, and yet we use worldly words and understanding to explain who goes to heaven and who goes to hell. We think because we go to church or get baptized, this secures us a spot in heaven, while Christ himself teaches that he went into churches to cure people because this is where sin and sickness is found. People should be able to go to church to get healed, but many times sick people stay sick because those leaders in the church are not willing to acknowledge truth but, instead, are false teachers. Being in church and being part of his church are two totally different things, which I hope that by reading this book, people will come to understand and acknowledge as truth so change can take place. I have seen many "successful" businessmen and women who have done me and other people wrong. Yet they are recognized by magazines and big well-known critics who decide their success. I have even confronted these people and received no response. They have no excuse, and they know nothing other than the man-made value system they have managed to climb to the top of that really means nothing of their actual success. They cannot even speak without staged remarks. What funeral have you gone to where you remember a funeral director saying, "Well, unfortunately, this man went to hell." I often wondered why funeral directors just say that the deceased was in heaven. How do they know? The fact is, this is just another distraction, worldly words and ideas to give people false hope and a fake sense of security so that no one needs to possibly suggest otherwise. The hope and prayer is that they went to heaven, but this needs to be prayed for and taken care of before someone dies, not after. That is why it is so important to give people time with their loved ones before they die and to pray with and for them. Sometimes people need that time. The Bible clearly states that not everyone who says, "Lord, Lord" will enter the kingdom of heaven. This is a decision of heart. This is a relationship between people and God. This is spiritual. If your spirit is linked with the spirit of another and you both know God and he knows you, you can believe that, as far as you know, that person is in heaven. It is hope that assures they are there. God gives blessed assurance of that. People, words, even actions cannot tell us for sure that someone is in heaven or hell. This is why our own relationship with God is most important. What we do in this life to be a "good person" according to the world's standards does not get us into heaven. What we do in this life as a "bad person" does not assure us a place in hell. If we can start understanding heaven and hell and the spiritual battle that every day calls us to, we will live a completely different life. Romans 10:9–10 states that if you confess with your mouth "Jesus is Lord and believe in your heart that God raised him from the dead, you will be saved."

Chapter 21

The Fight Is Bigger Than Just Where I Am

New York nurses were reportedly on strike around this time, and they walked out of a meeting held to come up with an agreement. They were asked why when offered more money, they still walked out and not settle, and they responded by saying this was never a battle to get more money but to have safer staffing for the nurses and patients. These nurses claimed that nurses in the ER had as many as twenty patients apiece, while the CEO of the company was making a fortune. They were asked if they felt guilty that patients were being rerouted to other hospitals for care since they were striking, and they said this was management's fault as they were told a long time ago about this crisis. It was bad even before COVID and only got worse because of greed. I remembered reading about how laws were established so that business owners could not monopolize to the extent of preventing appropriate competition. This was to prevent the business owner from gaining too much power over the consumer. I investigated this idea. A certain computer software engineer was trying to do this with his businesses years ago, and this was what pushed legislative moves. He called himself a philanthropist, someone who gives to charity, but there is information that supports the fact that he gave to charities that were started to force billionaires to give back some of their earnings. Guess who started this charity. The computer software billionaire himself, meaning that he gets money back from the very charity he started, making this a profitable organization. The more I learn about people with money, the more greed I find. The rich get richer, and they prey on everyone else. The world wants to be like these billionaires instead of frowning on their actions. This is nothing new. Look back at the story of Judas Iscariot, Jesus's disciple who later betrayed him. When the woman was using expensive perfume to wash Jesus's feet, Judas said that she should have sold that perfume and the money given to the poor. Jesus knew that Judas collected the money for the poor and took some for himself from the charitable money bags. Jesus knew this about Judas and knows this about all people who use this kind of trickery to gain for themselves. He told Judas to "leave her alone." Jesus told this timeless story to teach us that he knows about the dishonest people of this world and he protects us from them. He did not force Judas out of the group. He was still a disciple, and Jesus knew he would ultimately betray him; he just factored it into the plan and used it for good. He can do this with all things even when people are evil, so we don't need to fear anyone.

    I got a letter in the mail from our medical insurance company that stated that they were fighting with this very hospital chain in my area because they were raising their prices. Their prices were higher than average, something they were able to do because of how they were becoming so big in the area, and everyone who worked for them was forced to go to their facilities to get care since going elsewhere would have costed them an arm and a leg, being out of network. My insurance company said they would no longer cover any care at these facilities if this hospital chain was not willing to renegotiate. I did not have insurance through my work at the time; it was through my husband's job. People who had the insurance through my hospital had their own battles they fought, but this was the one I dealt with. My doctor was through this hospital system because his office was one of the ones bought over by them. All the hospitals in the area were too. They were allowed to capitalize, and I was wondering why our lawmakers and representatives were not putting a stop to this. If I was to become pregnant, this would have been a huge concern because the only maternity clinic in the area was owned by this company.

All the others went out of business. There were several who went out of business over the last eight years. That meant I would have to travel forty-five minutes to the next hospital to deliver a baby. It was a disservice they were providing to the community. What were they offering these doctors to be bought out by them? Why were the doctors in our area not fighting to be their own entity when this would have helped people to have choices? It was like the mafia or a game of monopoly with the best interest of the people not being a factor. Eventually, the big hospital chain did come to an agreement with the insurance company, and they settled. This gave my family more time, but I knew it would not be long before they would take over more and more if this evil was not stopped. Then this hospital chain would have the opportunity to further hurt people by not giving them an option for health care. I would be forced to move out of the area so that I could have medical coverage. This is why people need to do their good deeds and pay attention to what is going on in the community when an opportunity arises. Doctors were allowing this takeover. Did they know the power they had in God to put a stop to this kind of demonic influence? When we get comfortable in believing we are successful, we continue to make decisions that promote that kind of success. We have meetings with others who hold these beliefs too to promote the demonic influence, and the cycle continues. When we believe our success comes from glorifying God, which is to take care of his people, we understand the meaning of life, and we work to promote this kind of success. Otherwise, we are just like Judas, getting caught up in the devil's schemes, which is what was displayed by the hospital chain and not just in my area but all over the world. People were too busy self-soothing, taking vacations, and playing on their phones to pay attention or to make a change. They are tempted to just curl up to a romance novel and dream of another life instead of fighting for one.

Chapter 22

Why Are We Tolerating the Corruption?

To be a nurse today, business and making money for the lead people must be at the forefront of your thinking, or you will be beat down. I saw it in sports too. On the court with a girl who made certain obnoxious gestures after making a layup, gloating and instigating her opponents, the audience cheered, and the stands were full. They enjoyed this kind of activity on the court. It drew them in. They loved this disrespectful gloating, even though it was abuse of self that they were observing. Other basketball players did this too, and after my daughter's team, Army West Point, was out of the playoffs, I just stopped watching college and professional basketball altogether. Judas was disrespecting himself by ripping people off and taking money from the poor, but still he continued and wanted Jesus to promote his activity. The world is working hard to teach people to hate and abuse themselves while making the people at the top all the money. The big leaders are on vacation and relaxing, while the people doing the groundwork are busting their butts to keep things running. Why are people not standing up against this? People like it. They like the low standard and cutting corners to make a buck. They want a reason to drink alcohol, give up, or to just have something to complain about. People allow themselves to be victims of circumstance. People have even made a living out of making these very problems in nursing a joke. They travel around the world exploiting nurses by making jokes about how hard nursing life is. They're making good money making jokes about the abuse instead of working to stop it. Then nurses go to these functions, get a good laugh, and then go back to their jobs, being miserable. They live through their torment and then go home and read a fictional romance novel so they can escape, to take their minds off their failing love life and their abusive job that they hate. Where is the self-respect? They do not want to face the reality that they are responsible for their positions and outcomes in life. Regardless of what they are up against, they must find a way to do the right thing even when it is hard. This is a battleground, and we all could pick a side. This is not a task. This is a gift, to choose. If we sit around doing nothing, we are accountable. What did the woman do in the story? She worshipped Jesus and washed his feet with her hair and expensive perfume, even in the presence of Judas. She was not taking cushy jobs or off somewhere on vacation. She was waiting for Jesus to come, preparing for him, and when the opportunity finally came, she was there to wash his feet and carry out her hope to serve him amid her enemies. This is what we should be doing in the hospital, and this is what I will never stop doing. This is a choice, to acknowledge truth. I hope more people will speak up and make a change.

  This was happening in the school system, and the athletic director, some coaches, and people on the school board were worshipping demonic influence through what the world calls "conflict of interest." People in high positions in the school had kids who had good positions on sports teams at the school. Open enrollment gave the school the look of a charitable organization, but really they were Judas Iscariots. A principal at one of the schools pushed her son in front of my younger son while in line for pizza at a basketball event. She told my son that her son was on the varsity basketball team and was in tenth grade, so my son needed to let her son get in front of him to get his pizza first. He did get in front of my son after smirking at him and got his pizza before my son. This is the opposite of leadership. My son should have been able to look up to her son, but instead, he couldn't, and his mom was a poor leader as well. This is demonic teaching and is alive and well in the school system in my area. There are no evil programs, just evil people who invite the devil into their lives and worship him as they prey on others. The school system knew of this principal and that she acted like this. She thought she was better than everyone else. She had the nickname from the kids as "The Devil." When I told the athletic director this story, he already knew of this woman's reputation and told me he knew who I was talking about even though I gave no name. He said his hands were tied, and he could do nothing about it. Her son had no more talent than my oldest son, and yet he played on varsity while my son sat on the bench as a senior with years of experience on the team. She essentially abused both of my sons and taught her kids to as well yet was a principal at the school. Leaders overlooked their responsibility as men in these roles at the school. Their positions were sustained by God, but they believed their positions were sustained by the school board, so they played the games to stay in these "high-ranking" positions. They lived in fantasy believing they were good leaders. These people in the school pumped their chests up and were using the township's money to support a small number of kids—their kids or their family's kids. It was a cult, a mafia. People who came to basketball games who could not pay for a ticket or just did not know how, since we used a new electronic system that not everyone was familiar with, would be turned away from games. My dad caught many people at the door and paid for them so they could see their family member play in the game. Does this sound like a charitable organization? They were hypocrites. Extorting the kids and families to support a system that favored them in some way. They needed others to support them, so they made it seem to be something everyone wanted to be part of. "Feed the nest" was a saying they used to get people to trust them. I never supported this corruption but, instead, taught my kids to serve God first, then their teammates, not the system or the "nest" itself that makes absolutely no sense. Coaches are taking positions for reasons other than being passionate to lead kids in the right direction. This has been having a negative effect for generations. Why are we tolerating this? Adults have been finding more and more ways to worship self instead of bringing good to others and being responsible to raise kids right.

THE VOICE OF TRUTH

This is what I'm seeing in my area, and when I travel, I see it in other places as well, so I know the epidemic is spreading. It is worse than COVID because it effects the soul and spirit. God says these are the epidemics we should pay more attention to because they have eternal effects, and yet people do not get involved in making a change. It is everyone's job to get involved and learn ways to turn things around. I'm so thankful for the parents and coaches who are deciding to take a stand in this and give of themselves. It is not easy, and you will feel alone much of the time, but then again, if you are leading, who is in front or around you? To be a leader, you must be willing to walk ahead and focus on discipline for the sake of others. It will be worth it in the end.

Chapter 23

Fighting for Myself

On January 27, 2023, I had worked a twelve-hour shift. I had a total of eleven patients over the course of the day. I started with eight patients, which was too many in number and acuity as well. This assignment was four moms and four babies. One baby was withdrawing, so this baby needed to be assessed more frequently. Three moms were C-sections, and one was a vaginal delivery. All four moms were discharges and three of the four babies would be going home. The drug baby was staying because policy had us keep them for five days since they were withdrawing off drugs. After I discharged all my patients, I filled two more rooms. A vaginal delivery mom and baby and a C-section mom, whose baby went to NICU. The C-section mom was vomiting since her delivery, and they suspected she was having an allergic reaction to the opiate drug she received through her spinal morphine, so I had to put on a scopolamine patch right away and started her on a Narcan drip to slowly pull off the effects of the morphine. She was not feeling well, and I was not sure how soon she would feel better and what pain meds would be used after the Narcan began working, counteracting the pain relief of the pain medicine. I was hoping since it was a slow drip, it would ease her off the med slowly, but even still, would she tolerate pain meds? I was thankful to be leaving soon as my shift was ending in about three hours. I could not wait to get out of there.

    I decided to start fighting for myself. After eight years straight of being a per diem nurse and only getting, I think, one or two raises over that time, I decided to apply for a staff nurse position. That was what I needed for my family at that time. Once I realized how long I had let the hospital overlook my hard work, I knew I needed a change. I let my boss know I was seeking a part-time position. She responded back that she had no part-time positions available at the time. Later that week I went into her office and told her I would be looking for an additional job, part-time or full-time but that I still wanted to pick up shifts there to keep up my skills. She agreed that I could pick up shifts there but again never offered me a position.

That same day, I was very busy with a patient who needed a blood transfusion. With the heavy workload I had on top of the fact that my company refused to give me a raise in my current position or the lateral move to a position on night shift that would cause me to get paid a respectable wage that was far long overdue and could benefit my family, I was fighting. I needed this job on night turn, and I believed it would have made such a positive impact on my family. I know that with struggle comes strength and growth. God had something better for me, so I had to stay faithful through the storm. People strive to get into and then stay in these jobs of leadership because they can indulge in things like no weekends, no holidays, no night shifts. They did not get canceled from their shifts or pulled from their units to be forced to work in places that they were not comfortable in, but they would allow others to be put in these situations. What made them better? They easily shifted to the easier position even though that position represented putting others out. Our leaders would put others in situations all the time that they believed they were above being put in themselves. They were thieves just like Judas, keeping for themselves what they wanted and passing out little charity when and how they desired to and then taking credit for their work that they were so proud of believing they did. It was pathetic. They believed they had power in their title and position, but the reality was they could be displaced anytime. Why invest in something so temporary and in a position with no honor. I could not be part of it much longer, and God knew I was starving for more purpose. God could remove them from their positions of "power" anytime, and this was what we all need to recognize. James 4:14 says, "We do not really know about tomorrow. What is your life? You are a mist that appears for only a short while before it vanishes." Moral standards have been lost in corporate compliance. What sense did this make to have a person who believes they are in charge to walk around with a clipboard, checking on nurses who had more experience than they did? Their spirit was threatened by truth. I did not need checked on, and my capabilities and confidence in God put me at a level that prevented a person in this position who was freelancing their authority to be justified. That commitment to the corporeal world is no match for God. I was not looked out for by most of the people in this facility like Jesus looked out for the lady washing his feet. My circle is small, and this is okay. God keeps it small so I depend on him. This was why I was now able to see that I so desired to get another job where I could hope to find like-minded people who served God and who worked for something bigger and beyond corporate compliance. I was praying for this. I desired to be used by God, so I did not need to worry about the abuse and neglect by my leaders. This is what I want other nurses and people everywhere to understand. We are not under their power. We need to respect them as God does because people were made in his image, but they do not decide our lives or have control over our destiny, even our daily destiny. Continue to climb with God and leave corporate compliance in the dust. There is no life there. You can be in it but not of it. This is where we need to be—in the world but not of it. God is our source of direction in that. Keep striving and trust God to give you purpose either where you are or in another place that he can take you to.

I knew that my desire for nurses and patients to be treated with respect would cause me to have a target on my back, but now I was seeing a tangible representation of that in the fact that a new nurse could be offered a position over someone who needed no training at all and who could start right away. I was not offered the position. I was a respected nurse who was loyal and who had twenty years' experience in the field of nursing and fifteen years of experience in the field of mom and baby specifically. Once again, were they folding against their own policy and principles? Was this retaliation for speaking up?

Chapter 24

Learning How to Survive the Storm

Finally, basketball season was coming to a close for my daughter Sabria. We had senior night at West Point, and her basketball team was trucking along with lots of struggles on the court. They were battling refs who were trying to control the games instead of regulating them. This was so familiar to me because of what I was experiencing at work in leadership. I saw how Army basketball and Sabria just kept playing the game the way it should have been played, and for the most part, they were choosing not to get involved in the mischievous activities of their opponents who were trying to look a certain way, drawing fouls to get the call instead of relying on their talent and hard work to decide the game. I say most because not everyone was a supporter of truth, but most were. The refs played into this activity, and they had power on the court to change the flow of the game, and even though this was wrong of them, they indulged. Sabria was learning to stay honorable and focused on her task of living her own life with honesty and dedication to growing in basketball and in life instead of taking shortcuts to get the win on the scoreboard. When you get distracted and fold into the success of the world and dabble in shortcuts, so much is lost in the process including one's integrity and commitment to quality work. In turn, the quality of the game is tarnished, sometimes completely lost. Sometimes we feel like our efforts do not matter. However, Jesus taught us that we are not forgotten even though the world wants us to believe this.

I decided I still needed a job and found that what was going on at work was very similar to what I saw happening in basketball. Sabria's basketball career was rounding the corner and heading to the finish line. We had some things to take care of financially, and I just needed to stay focused and remain responsible for myself regardless of the leaders I worked with and how messy my unit and hospital was. There is so much power in finding yourself in a world with so many distractions. I had to just start taking some steps to grow, and the first thing I had to do was find a job, or so I thought. I began to understand that having a job for the sake of making money distracts people from their purpose, but I wasn't completely convinced yet. I learned so much from watching that Army Women's Basketball team from 2022 to 2023. They forged against the fire. They stayed honorable through the fight. I had sent my boss a text on February 15, 2023, asking for a full-time position on my unit. At that point I had faith, but it was just enough to make the moves I was making, and I believed I needed to work in that realm to earn a living. I was still being canceled and pulled off my unit to labor and delivery.

That very week that I applied, I was pulled off my unit and sent to labor and delivery. I had a woman who hemorrhaged during delivery and got a blood transfusion right before I got to work, and then I had a mom who had a C-section and was left on the cart in recovery. Recovery for C-sections was only about three hours, but she was left on the cart for double the normal time, about six hours, by the time I could send her to an open bed on postpartum. My other patient was in pain, and her blood pressure spiked right before I got there, and she only spoke Spanish. It always felt like I was entering an uncontrolled environment when I stepped on the floor, never knowing where I was going to work or what help would be available to me. I was used that day to relieve a unit that was not even mine, and it felt unstable all the time. That day, one of my leaders was over on the labor and delivery side, talking, and I wondered why she never asked me if my patients needed anything since I was pulled off my unit and had a heavy assignment with all freshly delivered patients, a bleeder, a surgical patient, and a non-English-speaking patient with high blood pressure. Did she know? Did she care? This leader would have to make time to walk around with her clipboard and ask the patients if I was doing my job because this was what she was told to do by her superiors, so maybe she just did not have time to check on me.

The hospital still would not expand the postpartum unit, and I wondered who was getting their big bonuses that year for keeping nurses at home, nurses underpaid, and patients left on carts and backed up on other units. I had written letters and exposed truth to everyone in leadership about this and even to state representatives and nursing support agencies, but little change took place. I did not hear back from our head either who was making the big money. In fact, what they wanted us to do was to work even faster by rushing patients out of the hospital before 11:00 a.m. and wanted us to ask the patients if they wanted to go home a day early. This made it possible to cancel nurses, which saved the company more money, but the nurses had to do everything they would normally do in two to three days in one or two days. This was why the nurses were exhausted and why my family was suffering financially, and yet I heard about how one of our leaders was looking to buy a new house and to take a vacation soon. Nurses were complying with this nonsense. Some did because they felt like they had no choice. Some could not find their voice, and some still trusted that they were somehow worth more in life if they helped this business gain more profit. Some nurses just decided to go back to school because if they got a higher degree too, like their leaders, they could be in charge and get out of this situation. Some were essentially jealous of the ones who were doing evil instead of fighting against the evil. I understood the perspectives, but I did not want any of it, and none of these options were for me. I worked hard fighting against the evil and kept finding myself moving against the grain. After I began speaking up about what was going on, I was convicted to tighten up and stay accountable to the quality of work I brought to the unit and to all areas of life. I wanted to be the exact opposite of what I saw represented. I craved discipline and self-respect. Part of the problem was the staff feeling like their hands were tied in response to this activity by our leadership and the corporation altogether. We all wanted to do a good job, but there was so much distraction, and the job became such a headache. I tried to be an example of someone who always loved and did not get involved in the evil, but it was just hard to be there. The leaders made a dry-erase board and set it in the nurses' station so we could all put on our patient's slot, why they were not discharged yet—whether it was because they needed a doctor's order, circumcision for baby, or ride. This was not to help the patient at all; it was to make more money for the company even though they were making the nurses work harder, faster, and without the help that was recommended for doing the job safely. Instead of having a nurse come in, they had a person with a clipboard going around and asking the patients if the nurses were doing their jobs the way they expected them to. They would ask them specific questions about what time the nurses came in their rooms and what they did while they were in there. Even though the leaders claimed they did not micromanage, but they did it to a tee. I heard that, finally, a patient's husband said that he was not there to evaluate the nurses doing their jobs; he was there to take care of his wife and baby and make sure they got home safe. He wanted nothing to do with the hospital's shenanigans. This kind of pressure from our bosses goes far up the chain all the way to the prince of darkness. He is at the head of this corporate compliance, so when you fight against it, you must fight spiritually. More people need to stand up and say no to this kind of abuse.

During this time of hoping to get a job on my unit, I had sent in a resume and got an interview with the recruiter and one of my leaders, and that was encouraging. This was after my leaders did not let me know of the open position that they were interviewing for on the unit even though I requested a more stable job than my per diem position there. I was still hoping for God to make a way for me to serve him while being faithful and trusting him to provide for my family. Sabria and Army West Point played against Boston U shortly before this all went on. In this game I saw the same type of discrimination I was seeing in the workplace. I understood so much after watching this game and not being given a job. Sabria specifically was shown dishonor in many ways. Every time Sabria would get fouled and the refs did not call it, or her opponents set up traps to catch her off guard so they could get an unmerited foul against her from the ref, she just went right back to business. It never stalled her or affected her progress. Sometimes it did affect the scoreboard, and they lost games over the discrimination, but she remained honorable through this and kept her focus on her mission to be a good example and to play the real game of basketball, the way it was meant to be played. She continued washing Jesus's feet in the midst of the Judases in the room, even though she still got blamed for lost games. She knew what was true. She self-reflected to change what should change about herself and looked at what she did right. This was congruent to my situation. I was seemingly losing at times, but God was my provider, and so we were always taken care of financially and otherwise. The devil uses money as a way for people to believe they are trapped in their jobs and circumstances, but we need to break free from these chains, and God was going to soon do this for me. As long as I stayed honest and remembered my mission to be a good nurse, bringing good care to patients and keeping nursing the way it was supposed to be, no harm would come to me. I lost nothing. I needed this mindset and the teaching from Army that night as they lost that game in overtime with this reportedly being possibly one of the most one-sided and offensively dominant overtimes in basketball history. They just ran out of steam as Boston was allowed by the regulators of the game to abuse Army and run them down, making them work harder than Boston with less reward. In the end, Army stayed honorable through the scheming. They did not win that semifinal game and were then out of the running for Patriot League Champions, but those who watched the game and knew basketball knew Army really won that game. I used what I learned from this to give my boss the time to make the decision to give me a position on the unit. If she chose someone else for the job, I would let God direct me elsewhere. I wanted to give leadership the opportunity to do the honorable thing in spite of the fact that they were probably encouraged otherwise by the company or, more specifically, the devil. I knew they did not want me there. I knew this based on the harassment I received form human resources and by the nurses not being heard or respected. They would retaliate against me by finding a way to delay me getting a job in hopes that I would leave. I already knew their schemes. "Delay, deny, deflect." My boss had the chance to support truth and to offer me a job that would pay me a fair wage that would support my family and that reflected my years of service to the company and to nursing. If she did not, I was prepared to leave. I did not want this job. I did not want night shift, but this was not about me. It was about my mission and about making a change and also being used by God where he saw fit. He closes and opens doors for us, and I really was excited as to what he would have for me. Whatever it was, I would do it with honor just like God taught me through Sabria. I would be thankful to make money for my family and to serve the community, and I would learn to stay up at night. If that door closed, I would apply for other jobs and look for the open door. Whatever it was, it was good.

    Later that week, over the weekend, I realized how nice it was to not have to worry about micromanagement. There was such good flow to the unit since there were no bosses present. It reminds me of how in basketball, the flow of the game can get interrupted by the refs, and the quality of the game gets lost if they are after control and not inspiring through the game. It is the same with nursing. I was taking care of a patient that day, a mom who had somewhat of an anxiety attack through the night. She was stressed out. The nurse took her baby and let her sleep through the night. When I came in the morning, I listened to her needs. I heard of her concerns and tried to follow through with her specific requests regarding her care. She was very anxious about breastfeeding. She vented to me and was honest about her plans for her husband to help with feedings at night and did not want to be judged for this decision. I explained that her perspective was respected by me, and I appreciated her honesty. I told her I would tell the consultant and that she was very nice and would have some good tips to help her if she changed her mind. I then had a conversation with her as I could see she was concerned, nervous, scared, and unsettled. I explained that part of having a baby is that you do not know all that will happen and that a lot of it is about having an open mind so that when things come up, it is not a scary or unexpected thing but more of a time to learn and grow. I talked to her in a way that helped her understand that her voice matters and her thoughts are valued. I shared some things with her based on my knowledge gained from having six kids of my own and breastfeeding, but I also used formula at times too. I knew that she would need to be flexible because she was a working mom. This would be tough. But I knew this tough. I wanted her to know that she was the one who knew her life, and she needed to be responsible for what was expected of her, and it sounded like she was being honest about what she would be experiencing.

I had a hard time when my kids were little. Back in that day not everyone got electric breast pumps for free from their insurance companies. I never owned one, and I worked as a nurse through those times and had insurance that I paid for through the hospital, and I was never offered an electric breast pump. They weren't covered under our insurance. I had manual ones that I bought myself with the money I earned from working in the hospital over those long shifts, and I still breastfed when I went back to work as I would pump on my breaks. Once I had an illness after delivering one of my kids. I had just delivered my third baby, and a day later I developed a rash all over my body. I had what was called PUPPPs. This led to engorgement, which was swelling and pain in my breasts because they were overfilled with milk. I found out I could not breastfeed because I had to be put on a steroid to treat the process going on in my body. I had to pump and dump while I was on steroids. I just remember being in a fog. I was so tired, sore, and the rash was unbearable. Plus I had three kids, and I was trying to figure that out. I had no pump at the time, since I threw out my old one, and I remember my dad came to my house and took me to the store because it was late at night when Bobby and I finally got the prescription for meds and got settled at home, and I did not want to go to the store alone in that condition. My dad was willing to help me shop for a breast pump. My dad was different. Was it weird shopping for this with his daughter? For a second, I felt bad that he had to be there with me, but I was so sick, itchy, and in so much pain I just knew I needed the help. I remember him picking up boxes at Walgreens and showing them to me. "How about this one? This looks like a good one. It says it is gentle and comes with extra bottles!" I laugh now because he was awesome. I was blessed with the best dad. I am sure he would have rather been doing anything else other than searching for a manual breast pump with his daughter, but there was nowhere he would rather be because I really needed the help and support, and he loved being that for anyone and everyone. Back then, fifteen years ago, family still took care of family, and I was taught that nothing is free except salvation through Jesus. I learned a lot through these tough times. I was given a passion for people. People were not always honest or understanding, so what I tried to do is to be this for everyone. I didn't think I was very good at it, but I tried. We do not all go through the same struggles, but we can learn how to relate to everyone if we try. My dad taught me that even if I do not completely know the whole subject matter, I can still be exactly what people need, just like when he was there for me that night as we frantically shopped for a pump that could give me some much-needed relief while I was healing.

Chapter 25

My Dad and Why He Is My Hero

My past built me for all I would go through in raising my kids, handling my marriage, and the position I had at work. Growing up, I could remember that our house was the hangout. Back then, in the eighties, we played outside. My dad made us a homemade tetherball, and we were the only house in the neighborhood with a basketball hoop. All the kids came there to play. My dad worked so many jobs. He was an auxiliary police officer. He would not take a job full-time at the department because it would be a drop in pay from his other job, and he could not afford it, but he loved to serve in that way, so he stayed on the force. He had other jobs too—security, landscaping, factory jobs, to name a few. He was always working to financially support our family, and when he was home, he made such an impact. This is where I learned balance even in tough times; it is possible. All the kids came to our house in the evening for a big basketball game, and my dad would be busy making hot chocolate in a giant pot on the stove for all of us. In the winter he made big snow forts in the backyard, and we'd have the best snowball fights. The kids came over, and all got into it. They were mostly kids from broken homes. Our neighborhood was on the west side of Youngstown. We were all people who were trying to get by. There was divorce, drugs, gangs, and murder very close by and in that neighborhood, and my dad wanted people to know there was another way. The kids all went through things at home, but many did have love in their hearts. They needed to see something other than what they saw every day in the bad. They needed to see a contrast to the chaos. They needed to see more of Jesus and less of Judas. One day we heard about our friend a few houses up the street. His mom's boyfriend was shot dead in the street. I was young and just remember it being called a domestic. His blood stained the street for weeks, and as we rode our bikes past that house, there was a sense of reverence, I felt, for the whole situation. I knew that people were hurting. I knew not every family lived like mine and had support and love around them, but the kids in the neighborhood were important to my dad. Everyone was. He was tough too when he needed to be. I found out when I was older that my dad, after his police days, would go to the prisons and minister to the inmates. He wanted them to know the truth and about God. He loved everyone, and he taught me this love.

One day, as a child, I went screaming to my dad as I saw a group of boys running down the street with my new trick bike. I was frantic, but my dad acted quick and chased down those thieves. He caught up to them after chasing them down the street and over the railroad tracks by the mill. He caught the little one, who was maybe seven years old. The other older kids kept running off with my bike. He held up the little boy and said, "Hey, do you want your little brother back? Bring back the bike." They stopped running and looked back. They paused and headed back to my dad with their heads down and gave the bike back, and he let their little brother go, and they walked away together, hopefully learning a lesson of humility and exercising loyalty that day. They were not from our neighborhood. They probably came over from the North side or maybe the projects near my house. They just came to steal, but my dad protected us and let those kids know he was not there to punish them but to demand respect and expected them to respect themselves. They valued their brother over the bike, and they proved it that day. This is what he wanted them to see and me too. Putting people over things was the lesson. My dad let them all go unharmed and did not get the police department involved. Teaching morals and values was important to him, and we have this power too if we serve God. He did not use his police badge to abuse people. He used it to teach discipline, law, and respect for self and others. He believed in God's justice.

I remember another time when we were playing backyard football at the neighbor's house. They had a nice long yard, just like a football field. It was a kind older couple, Greek Orthodox, who lived there. We had to respect their yard, and we knew that, and they let us play there as long as we were good. I had my hamster, Zipper, out that day, and taking a break from football, my friend, a boy from up the street, asked me to let him hold him. The boys started getting rowdy and began tossing my hamster back and forth between them, and I told them to stop, but they were laughing and continued horsing around, pumped with adrenaline from the game. My hamster, being afraid, bit the boy on the hand, and this stunned him, and he yelled out, "Ouch!" He then let the hamster go mid-toss, and I watched him just fly through the air and then plop onto the grass. I screamed and ran to him. He was bleeding out of his mouth and was breathing fast. He seemed to have a seizure, and then everything stopped. I watched him die. I was about eleven at the time. I was devastated and in shock. I felt responsible. He was my pet. I should have protected him. The boys were in shock too and did not know how to respond. One minute they were laughing and playing, and the next minute they killed someone's pet. I ran home crying. For days I would not talk to the boy who did this. He was a few years older than me, and the other kids in the neighborhood told me he could not believe what happened and did not want to face me. He was telling them to beg me for his forgiveness and to let me know he was so very sorry. I wanted to forgive him but needed him to never do this kind of thing again.

One of the other boys from the neighborhood came over as I was preparing the old cigar box my grandpa gave me that would be Zipper's casket. I wrote a note on the box and laid him in there. The boy, who was about my age, just stared into the box at the dead hamster as we had a moment of silence. I remember his chubby hands and his oversized ripped sweatshirt and how kind he was to be in that moment with me. I figured he had a rough home life, but he was sweet. I buried the box. I was thankful for the company and the boy's softness toward my pain and toward what happened to my pet. I thought for a while and then told the neighborhood kids to tell the other boy I would forgive him, but he needed to do something for me first. He needed to come over and clean out the hamster's cage. This was always a job I hated doing. It was smelly and a gross job to me. It would be extra hard doing this job now since I was not making a nice home for Zipper but only cleaning up a mess. Plus I knew this boy liked to look and smell good. His dark gelled hair was always combed, and his leather jacket finished off his Italian Stallion look. If he was willing to clean out this dirty, smelly hamster cage, he must really be sorry. I was impressed when he showed up for hamster cage cleaning duty. He looked at me and said he was sorry and explained that when the hamster bit him he was caught off guard and released him into the air. As he told me the story, I could see in his big brown soothing eyes that he really felt bad. It was an accident. I understood. I had my head down thinking about what happened to Zipper, and then he asked me to forgive him for what happened. I told him it was okay and that I forgave him. He really needed to hear that. He smiled and seemed so relieved. I smiled too. He said, "So are we good?" I said, "Yeah, we are good." He was not very good at cleaning, but I would not hold that against him. After all, I was tough. I was capable. I didn't really need the cage cleaned. I could do it myself. That day I wanted to do like my dad and see the good in a bad situation and let someone else see it too, so that is what I did. Together we learned forgiveness. I had to forgive him, and he had to forgive himself for what happened.

I loved these neighborhood kids. There was so much diversity there. We saw all kinds of kids living there—Black, White, Italian, Mexican, Puerto Rican, Greek, Polish, and Pakistanis. All different ages, but we all played together. Kids would always ask to eat dinner at our house, and my mom was always feeding more than just her own kids. We learned to connect through sports and playing outside. We went home when the streetlights came on. We hurt each other at times but learned to make up. We took the good with the bad. It was a great neighborhood. I appreciated life and learned about death. I learned to watch my back and the backs of my friends in that neighborhood. Having things like theft and murder in the area taught us to be careful. Knowing there was a dead body found, bound and wrapped up in a black trash bag on the side of the street, just around the corner from where you live, makes you learn how to watch your back. This was where I first learned the difference between good and evil, in this neighborhood. So now that I was grown, I found a new war zone. Coming from this kind of neighborhood, I learned to look out for violent people, but here at the hospital, I learned about a different kind of evil. The one inside the people with two faces. The one with the fake smile and a suit and tie. The one carrying a clipboard asking you how you are while patting you on the back but working to keep you in a bad situation. This was all too familiar to me. They would steal my bike in a heartbeat, just like those little boys did, but they would do it when my back was turned, and they would still smile at me later, pretending to comfort me when I told them the story of someone stealing my bike and maybe even offer me some homemade cookies. That was who these people were. They were snakes in the grass, and I knew about their scheming. They think they hide from people. They think their sins are camouflage, but if you have seen demons before, you recognize them even when they try to hide in people with worldly titles and reputations who do not live in the poor neighborhoods and carry guns. They live in the rich neighborhoods and carry arrogance and self-righteousness. All through my life, I have seen evil, all different kinds, and this helps me to recognize it and fight it. Just like Jesus told the world about how he knew Judas stole the charity money, Judas thought he got away with his scheming. Jesus knew Judas would betray him and told the world about it before it even happened. Still, he loved Judas and even let him be part of his group.

Later, after being in that hospital room, talking to and encouraging the anxious woman who was worried about breastfeeding and about transitioning at home, the patient's mother met me in the hallway. She thanked me for the conversation I had with her daughter. I could have these conversations because God built me over the years to connect with people. This woman said that there was so much wisdom in what I said to her daughter and that it was so helpful and exactly what she needed to hear. She said she was so glad I was the nurse who was there that day. She said that I could not even imagine how much of an impact my words made, but I knew. I have had people do that for me, and it has made all the difference in my life. This was the experience that I brought to the table for the patients. I knew I had much to offer and that my presence could bring power to people's lives because of the life I had and all that I had encountered through God. He showed me who he was in me and the impact he could make on others by working through me. This was all him. I did not know if leadership would decide that they valued me enough to give me the job. I knew they did not care about these values in a nurse. In fact, my values contrasted their mission.

My dad showed up at my house after I got off work on what would have been my mom's birthday. I had a long hard shift and he said he thought I needed a hug. How did he know?

Chapter 26

Hurry, Hide the Cups!

That same week, a boss came to the nurses' station in a panic. A leader came up to me and said, "Hurry, put all the cups away. Here they come, they are coming down the hall right now!" I just hurried and did what the leader said, hiding all the cups. I never worried about cups being out. If they had lids on them, we were allowed to have them out. That was a new rule, probably since nurses had bladder problems from being dehydrated at work, but she was so afraid and careful to impress these people. I had the leader's back and tried to ease and calm nerves by putting the cups under the cabinet, very quickly. We did not always have warning that the "suits" were coming, but here they were, showing up unannounced. It was the higher-up leaders and a group of businessmen and women from an outside company that would be taking over the housekeeping/cleaning department, I believe. They were looking around and getting a tour by the leaders. I saw a man from leadership in the crowd who acted like he was a man of power but never followed through on anything. He had a big title, though, and took lots of vacations. I had emailed him about a week before seeing him that day. In the email, I explained that I was applying for a job on the unit and wanted to further invest myself in that department to make a change. I explained that since my meeting with him back in September 2022, there had been some positive changes on the mom and baby unit, but they were minimal and temporary and more needed to be done. The nurses had thanked me for reaching out on their behalf. They said that their assignments had been less heavy at times and more manageable on many days, proving that a better unit was possible. As we strongly suggested, an LPN had been hired finally to help in the nursery, and I was honored that my coworkers thought of me as an advocate and a liaison between them and leadership in times of trouble. She was only per diem, though, and being per diem myself, I knew we would not utilize her as she was needed. I explained that since it was the nursing staff who drove the change and not leadership and that the changes we saw were not consistent, this meant they were possibly not permanent changes and that things could change for the worse at any time. In the last meeting, I was told by leadership that I brought up many problems but that I did not list any suggestions for change and that I needed to do homework. I hoped that now it was seen that our suggestions were there in the letter after all, and they did make an impact on the unit after we pushed for them to be implemented. There was still a lot more work to do, but I wanted to remain transparent with leadership by communicating this with him, and I wanted them to know I would be watching, making sure these changes were made more permanent. He never responded to my email. The hospital liked to do little things to shut up the complainers, but often the changes would not stick. Consistent growth is a characteristic of a true leader, and these people did not have it. I saw him that day in the crowd and was unimpressed. As I looked at this group walking down the hall, it reminded me of the group of businessmen walking down the hall, passing Chevy Chase in his office in the movie *National Lampoon's Christmas Vacation* when he is holding his coffee cup and they all looked like robots following each other. These were people with big worldly titles walking down the hall, making decisions for all the people doing the actual work. They should be regulating the place, not controlling it. Just like in basketball, with the refs and coaches, sometimes these people take over power, and instead of letting the real game play out, they sometimes end up micromanaging everything, and the quality of the game is lost. Talents and gifts are swallowed up, and we all end up at a loss, even the ones who get to take lots of vacations, buy big houses, and have their pockets full at the expense of others. They are not gaining anything good because as God tells us, it is worthless. They lose in the end. There are names for the people in these groups such as clipboards, suits, clowns, bots, and the like. These were the people my leader feared and just dashed to do something that made no sense, to put everyone's cups away so they would not see, and then acted like normal when they went by. I just sat there in my chair, proud of the fact that I was not afraid and that I knew what and who they all were. I may have not been able to change them or the place, but I could influence others to be better for themselves and to have a sense of self-value, knowing they are from God and work for him and through him in these institutions. I would continue to send emails and speak truth about what was going on, but I took no responsibility for the arrogance represented there. Let it be their own downfall if they have so many chances to change but choose to remain out of touch with reality.

    I finally got called into my boss's office and was told that she was interviewing me for the position I applied for, full-time night shift. My coworkers questioned me on this. They asked me why I needed an interview? Why did I need to submit a resume, apply online, meet with the human resources rep, and have an interview there as well? I said I didn't know. Although we all knew why. I had asked to be told when a position was available but was not told about this one. I found it online and had to apply for it as if I was from the outside. They would be going against their own principles if they were to hire someone from another floor or from outside when I had nineteen years of seniority and fourteen years in that unit specifically. They couldn't do that, but what they could do, they would. I had waited, and by the next week this was now a couple of weeks since I applied and several weeks since the position was posted. I was not sure why this process was so slow except that I knew God was working behind the scenes. He was the reason I saw the posting for the position in the first place. I did not know a position was available since the leaders knew I wanted a job but never told me about the position.

    On a Tuesday, March 21, I got the call from human resources offering me the position on my unit for full-time night shift. It was exactly as I expected, ten dollars more an hour than what I was making at the time. I also was offered a fifteen-thousand-dollar sign-on bonus. I accepted the position with a two-year contract, but the kicker was that they would not let me start until June 4. I said, "Oh wow, that is over two months away." The recruiter also thought this was odd and said she could text my boss and ask if I could start sooner since I really hoped to start working ASAP, and it was a parallel move, which meant since I already worked there, I should have been able to just start right away. That was the routine and what other nurses did all the time. I waited for the recruiter to call me back, and Bobby and I were praying. He never liked praying out loud but this time took a stand for me and our family. He prayed that a hedge would be around us and that we would be protected throughout this time. I was praying that God's will would be done and not mine. He had all the answers, not me, and he proved to have better plans than I did. Then the recruiter called back, but instead of telling me that I could start right away, she told me that the position was on hold now, and they were no longer offering the job to me. I could not believe my ears. What changed in the last half hour? She told me she was sorry and that my boss would call me and explain. I think she was out of the loop, and since I applied from this angle, she probably didn't know what was happening on my unit. This recruiter said she would keep my paperwork and that the position was mine as soon as it was taken off hold.

    I got off the phone and wondered what all the confusion was about. She congratulated me, and I accepted the position, only to have it taken away from me. They did not want me to have this job. I knew they did not want me making more money or being around more. They did not want me getting anything I asked for or having a more permanent position. But this was not them I was fighting against. This was a spiritual battle against oppression, against control, against self-righteousness, and against greed. It was also a time to know that Jesus was in control of my life, of my job, of my wage, of my finances, of my family, of my safety, and of my enemies. I moved on God's guidance to apply for this job, to send a new resume, have an interview, and to speak several times on the phone and through emails and texts with the recruiter over the last two weeks, and now nothing? Once again, my time was of no value to them. They offered something to me they were not even going to give me. I decided to remain unmoved from my position in faith to trust God. They had an opportunity to do something good for me and my family, and that opportunity was given to them by God who holds all authority. If they wanted to toy with that, I was not worried. God was my provider anyway, and I believed he was protecting me from taking this job because he had better plans. They should have given me opportunities long before this. I was pushing for opportunities now, and they still were pushing against me. I knew confusion was the work of the devil, and by the leader or representative of the company not calling me that night to explain the situation, it was obviously not of God. Why would they let me sit at home and be confused over the whole situation: have an offer, be given a job, and then have it taken away? I really wasn't confused, but it was so fitting for who I knew them to be, and I recognized this spirit of miscommunication and chaos, which was contrary to God. They were consistently inconsistent with information, treatment of others, plans, and execution. This hospital was always a place of unorganized chaos, and I was learning a lot. God kept me at peace and aware of where my focus needed to be. It was always God who held the power, and we can ask him to use us if we are faithful, or we can let opportunities pass us by. This is what we do have control of, our will. He will lead me to success anyway but gave them an opportunity to be willing to be part of his plan and receive blessings. I could not be angry or upset in any way. I was excited to see the doors he would open for me. After I decided to take this job and was willing myself to be obedient to his calling, I did find out that even though leadership knew of the weeks of interviews being done for this position and that the job opening had been online for several weeks, it was not until my name was put down and pushed through the system as the one receiving the job that the hiring freeze went into effect, and my immediate leader was forced to rescind her offer to me. The higher-ups used the excuse that they had not met their production numbers and their FTEs were off. Why did they interview several people for this job over several weeks and have the job posted in the first place? Once again, profit over people was their motto. This was an empty and lame excuse to put out a hiring freeze because our numbers were chronically off, and we were always getting lectured on how we needed to move better and faster and work with less to support the budget. So why now was it preventing me from getting a better position? It was an excuse they knew they could cover because our numbers were off. It was a way to cover their sin, but God had me covered, and he was preparing something for me even while this was going on. Were they retaliating? There were several new employees and even a friend of mine had recently moved from per diem status to part-time with seemingly no issue at all. I knew my faith was being tested. Was God enough for me? Could I trust him even through this?

My husband was not as strong as me, and I was always the leader of the family. I prayed for him to take this role. I did not want it and knew he should be in charge. This is God's natural order, but it always fell back on me. Bobby was putting the financial burden on me and wanted me to just find a job anywhere. He did not see me as a person either, just a paycheck. A means to an end. I had made lots of money in my life, but still God was the one who made it all possible for my needs to be met, and he would still do that for me. I was done breaking my back and slaving all day and night, only to end up here, unappreciated and abused by this company. My husband was very comfortable wasting money and even gambling whole paychecks away because I was his safety net. No more. God said I had done enough. I would not grasp at straws and just apply all over the place or wait for these people who hated me to give me a job. I was a leader, and leaders use logic, reasoning, and most of all, godly counsel. I needed to be used in a bigger way, not to make money per se. I hated money anyway. God was my provider. I wanted to do something with purpose, something to help the world be a better place. I needed to live life with passion and to also have more freedom to use my gifts and talents to better serve. This was my heart and my prayer. I needed some hope and to know relief was coming. This was where I would start coming alive.

Chapter 27

The Day I Would See My New Life

God would waste no time. I got a call that weekend on Friday night, March 17, from a friend who had been a coach for one of my kids in basketball. She let me know that the owner of a gym in our area was opening a new space. It was an old CrossFit gym. I took my jump stretch certification class a few years back hoping to one day use it. Coach Carl knew I was interested in coaching but had no idea how it would come about. My sister and my dad had both told me that jump stretch was the angle I needed to look at. They believed it was what I needed to do to make a difference and help people, and this had been brought up to me over the last couple of years. I just saw no way of doing it, and no door of opportunity was opened until now.

  I got involved in jump stretch eight years before this and learned the HIIT program using rubber bands to build strength, speed, flexibility, and agility and to prevent injury in sports and in everyday life. I quickly realized it was a way to teach kids about having good health, becoming stronger, faster, and safer athletes, with the bonus of training them about the moral principles of life. I was eager to train and be involved even more after my daughter was injured at West Point in basketball, tearing her ACL. My family saw how devoted I was to being an advocate for athletes, so this was a fit. Coach Carl used phrases like "the more you sweat in practice, the less you bleed in battle" and "the only place that success comes before work is in the dictionary." My gift of writing was very helpful to develop a program to build character and to give support for recovery, restoration of mind, body, and spirit after injury, and to give hope. I was intrigued to learn all I could and did write extensively about jump stretch in my first book that I published in 2021.

There were so many benefits I saw to this program by teaching kids during the class to use what God put inside them to battle things like anxiety, fear, poor self-esteem, and laziness, and to have a respect for themselves and others. People were encouraged by their own efforts in class, which gave them confidence to apply and stay committed to grounded morals that they believed in by seeing all they accomplished through jump stretch workouts. By coming to class when it was raining and cold and would rather have stayed inside, resting, they were committed to mind over matter. When they came to class when it was warm and sunny out instead of being selfish, goofing around, and soaking up the sun for that hour, they learned humility. They came when they were tired or when they had lots of homework, and this taught them fortitude, perseverance, and selflessness. It was a hard class, and it pushed you to your limits, and this made you feel like part of a team. Even in class when you knew nobody, you would slap the other athlete's hands and say "good job" because you knew how hard the work was. It built comradery among the people in the room. It was an understanding among people, and this was brought through athletics. The lessons learned were able to be used outside of that class and could be applied to everyday life, building good character, and this was what was needed to break down and then rebuild and reshape the understanding and ideas involved in corporate compliance. I could change it from the outside, from the ground up. I could help develop minds that were eager to be part of a team and understood and recognized hard work and were willing to take part and to encourage others to do this, maintaining a good attitude and reflecting good attributes of heart.

I often wondered how I could further invest in the program. I had taken the jump stretch class and enrolled all six of my kids in it because it was family-oriented, from ages ten and up. They all benefitted from it and even were heard quoting Coach Carl's phrases before tournaments or games. It was therapy for my son Quintin's anxiety, and it was confidence for my daughter Sabria to return to the court after ACL surgery and recovery. We all took the classes together, and all could compete individually but in the same class, building bonds that were able to cross over the barriers of age. It opened our minds to the idea that if we can cross that barrier, we could cross other barriers too that we once thought was holding us back, and this gave us power to demolish strongholds, building our faith in God. I was not ready then to coach, but I was now. I was a nurse and had done circuit training since I was a kid. I appreciated the body and even designed my own workouts. Now I knew why I spent all those years building my exercise dictionary in my head. I had a wide range of knowledge, and I was ready to be a jump stretch coach, bringing the unique quality and skill set that I gained over the years through nursing, sports, and my kids' injuries.

    I was ready for the call I got that Friday from my friend who told me that she had also recently talked to Coach Carl about teaching jump stretch, and he had mentioned me to her about wanting to do this. The three of us had been talking separately and having the same idea. I had been praying for something to work out and doors to be opened and people to help network through the process of this becoming possible. She told the guy opening the space about us teaching jump stretch. He loved the idea. I heard her saying all this, and it hit me in the heart, complete confirmation that I needed to do this. She asked me if I would be willing to get involved to teach the classes with her. I said, "Of course!" She had talked to the guy, and he said he had all the equipment we would need and was willing to get any additional equipment we would need to do the classes. He just really wanted fitness instructors to occupy the space, and he loved our ideas. We met with him the very next day at an open house for the gym, and my friend and I started brainstorming. It was exactly what I needed to move forward with teaching sports at a higher standard and with moral principles to give people a firm foundation in athletics and a quality program. We would create a big brother/big sister atmosphere. We would train kids up to respect themselves and to respect others and to be real teammates, which would hopefully continue into adulthood, creating better work and home environments than what I was seeing in the hospital. I had met so much resistance in the school system and at work with trying to promote change, and I knew this was the answer. To make my own environment where kids could come and see contrast between good and evil just like my dad did for the neighborhood kids growing up. I could take my kids out of the school system, but what about all the other kids who were there who could not leave? I wanted to do something for all kids and all people. I figured I would teach them how to have the mindset to be able to withstand the Judases in life and to still serve God in their presence. I would teach them what God taught me. I could do it while training them in sports using the best circuit, strength, and conditioning training system I had ever come across.

God was moving. I had started another book and had about five books that I was writing at that time. God was developing me and building me into who I would become, and this hospital and their shenanigans were so small to me. I realized how big God is in our lives, and this helped to demolish the stronghold of fear that I fought in moving on and venturing on to new and unchartered waters. I had a future, and I had purpose. I knew too much to stay where I was. God had developed me, and I needed to now teach what I knew. It was time to move on. I outgrew the hospital and those leaders with no vision. There was such a contrast between networking with people who believe in God and live by faith versus networking with the world and people who live by an algorithm. The difference is that with God, there is no confusion, misleading, or lying. There is no competition to be more "successful" than others because he has plans for us all. It is smooth, open, and all on the table. There is freedom to live and to grow and flourish. It is completely different. The world is about growing status, money, and selfish desires. They are experts in usury. I was excited to let God grow me as a person, his masterpiece, and in turn to use me to help build up others. I was uninterested in worldly stipulations, guidelines, and empty promises. I was not waiting for my boss to call me. I was trusting that God already had the plan mapped out, and when he opened the door, all I had to do was walk through it. The sky was the limit, and I had no idea about all that I would be doing next, but I knew it would be good.

My boss did call and said she was sorry about giving me a job and then taking it back. She tried to make up for it by saying that I could pick up extra time when it got busy. She told me to schedule my shifts for June still as a per diem nurse. So ultimately, she gave me a better job, and then demoted me, and then asked me to schedule shifts to fill the voids on the unit and to continue to work at a substandard pay. It was amusing that this company could stoop so low. They knew I had more seniority than the others they were giving opportunities to, but they did not care. I was so amused. To imply that I had not invested enough while working for that company for nineteen years and working every shift imaginable, doubles after doubles, on call, and nights year after year was ridiculous. I follow God, and this is why he is above all policy and procedure. Humble yourself and let God lift you up. You must be brave through this time. It will seem like you are losing, but you're not. I was afraid to teach jump stretch, especially when I had the best coach in Carl. How could I ever be good enough? However, Carl taught me through the classes that I was good enough. He taught me that people follow courage, not titles. He taught me to have the heart of a lion. My friend told me she was afraid too, and we both fought our fears and trusted God to teach through us. That was the only way it would be successful.

The world's system is a weak system, and there was no respect represented. Leadership was freelancing their authority in my company. It wasn't just here, though. While people were fighting for our country, our communities, and our families, others were getting rich making videos and taking selfies of the new bodies they created while in the gym during COVID pandemic. It was labeled as humility. People were posting pictures of themselves in provocative poses and calling it a good focus on self-image when it was feeding perversion. These were the athletes kids were told to look up to. As there was now a way for athletes to market themselves and make money off their name, they were going crazy trying to get attention, and this was making them millions. Gloating on the court, antagonizing opponents were all for one thing, to be popular. It was like the whole world was back in high school. The immature was now in charge of the country. It was hard to see, and it was an attempt to make a mockery out of me and every other service member. The basketball groups even nationally were calling these people leaders. It fed and fostered an environment for more dysfunction on the court. It caused less chemistry between teammates and more self-worship but was labeled as something to cause team bonding. Now the athletes were not concerned with being different in terms of good character but rather in becoming famous and popular, liked. They were even holding seminars promoting this as leadership and good character. It was the new trend where image and likeness are king. This is Antichrist activity, and it thrived in the sports world, especially basketball. I was shocked at how streamlined this all became. I was pushing hard in the opposite direction promoting purity and truth, while these huge groups who had these giant platforms were just ushering in floods of bad information and lies about good mental health and calling making bad decisions having positive lifestyles. All this was geared toward the physical body and the mind, and this was standing out to me. No one talked about the spiritual side. It was all bad. It pushed everyone into being empty, just a shell of a person with no faith in God, and this was feeding the mental health crisis, not helping it. This was another attack on our country, and the big, wealthy organizations were ushering in the enemy. I was so disappointed with the weakness represented in the sports world. I would work to do the opposite, not to fight them but to just push out the good news of truth and how to treat your body as a temple and to be an authentic leader, not an impostor.

 Chronological age does not mean you are trustworthy or knowledgeable, and worldly seniority is a fantasy value system, just like popularity on social media. My years of service and wisdom was not valued by the company, but God saw me, and he appreciated all my hard work. He was working things out for me as I walked in faith through this life. This was why he had me being bold and speaking truth so he could build me for my next mission. Working nights would be fine if that was what he had for me. It would open my schedule up to teach more jump stretch classes to be a true resource to people in sports and to be more flexible and adaptable to change. This company and the sports world were just such a disappointment, but God was a beautiful contrast to the ugliness. I signed up for extra shifts because leadership said I could work these until the job they gave me became available again, but then they opened the extra shifts to everyone, which means I was still not getting work. They were trying to snuff me out, but I had to remember this was the devil that was trying to hurt me, not people. God will always be bigger than the devil, so there was nothing to fear. The letdowns from the hospital leadership continued, but I continued to smile. I had some help from my dad who was there when I had my breakdowns, like when I had to miss important events for my family because I was scheduled to work, and then I would get canceled. I would call him, and he would remind me that God was big and my problems were small. I couldn't wait to move on from this, but I had to be patient.

When I got to work after all of that, learning of the job that I got and then had it taken and had a new opportunity with jump stretch, my coworkers from night shift all congratulated me. They all told me they heard I was hired and coming to nights, and they were so happy. I do not know how they knew or found out so fast, but somehow, they knew and heard the news. For the next couple of days, I continued to get congratulated, and I had to tell them that the job was taken away from me right after it was given, and they could not understand because it made no sense, but they just rolled their eyes as they expected nonsense from our company. At least I knew the staff valued me as a coworker. They knew I fought for them and that I did a good job and had their back. We had so much talent there and great nurses who put up with a lot and worked hard. They were growing from all that had happened, and they were also searching for something else other than what they saw in that place. This was so much better and richer than what was worshipped in our country. I was excited to know I could possibly end up working with them on night shift when the hiring freeze was lifted. I figured as soon as I quit or got a job on another floor, the hiring freeze would probably be unfrozen, but I decided none of the options meant anything to me. It was good to know God was in control of my life. We, as nurses, may not have been valued by that leadership, but I could show them how leadership could really be, which is to understand who you are to God, and to him you are worth everything. It is my honor to make the other nurses see for themselves that the sky is the limit and they too can know their own worth and climb higher and do greater things even without the recognition of their company leaders. That is what I aim to do, to help them realize they are the only one of them. They are not a number or a title with a level of seniority. They are God's masterpiece. This is what will bring them their passion and motivation to continue to work hard at work and in every area of their lives.

My husband and I were desperate for God's wisdom and guidance during this time. My dad and my sister really supported me through this time. I needed to walk in faith and not to break my back forever at a job that was disrespectful but, instead, to use the wisdom God gave me and to go where he led me. It was time to move on to bigger things where I could continue to make a change. The sports world was a mess, and I had to be tough to be able to enter that as I would end up finding out that it was cutthroat. I was ready, though. All my training through this process being an advocate had built me to take on the giants. I told Bobby that we were in the belly of the whale just like Jonah. God wanted Jonah's attention, and he wanted ours too. He let Jonah get swallowed up by a whale, and for days he lived in the belly of that fish. We knew it would not be easy in the belly, and it would be smelly and gross, but through that experience, we would learn. Bobby and I needed to stop depending on a world that would never take care of us. I knew times would be tough, especially financially, but we were not made to work our lives away, constantly grinding to make that dollar. We wanted more and not more schooling or more money. We wanted to invest our lives in things that had eternal value, like people. Truly invest in them and not the way the world did because that was so cheap and powerless. Kids would learn nothing and be empty learning what was being taught in the sports world. We had our oldest graduating college and our son graduating high school all in the next couple of months. Plus I was venturing onto a brand-new mission and adventure as a jump stretch coach. I had to believe what I told people, that the sky was the limit. I was more broke, financially and emotionally, than I had been in a long time, possibly the most broke I'd ever been and with certain things telling us it could be this way for a while, and yet I was so at peace. Not at first, though. At first, I ugly-cried after finally breaking down at what was going on in my life and feeling overwhelmed because I could only see the storm. I called my dad who had to give me a pep talk and tell me that I was amazing, and why was I down? He reminded me of all I had been through and all I still had to do and that it had nothing to do with making money. He was right, and I knew it. I was so hardworking, always giving a hundred percent, and I really was thriving. I was learning more than ever about who I was and all the plans God had for me. I believed in people, and I had to keep believing. So once I felt bad for myself and would cry at the drop of a hat and got that out of my system, God gave me this peace. He was taking me to a level that did not start and end with permission from other people. I had to learn that. No one had control of where I was going, except God. This is the heart of a fighter.

I also had recently found out that my oldest son's girlfriend was pregnant, meaning I would be a grandma, and my oldest Sabria told us that she was offered a position in Germany to start her career off as an army officer. She was given this opportunity, which was considered a high honor. She was told this would challenge her, especially with the language barrier. She would be just a short train ride away from several different countries in Europe such as Italy and France and could take day trips to these places, giving her opportunities she only dreamed of as she served her country. She was proud and honored to work to give others the opportunity to thrive. She was scared at first, but then once she accepted the posting, she was excited. Included in this arrangement was the hope of the possibility to continue her basketball career overseas. She was open-minded and wise beyond her years. She gave me hope. This offer to go to Germany as her placement as an ESEO (Environmental Science Engineering Officer) specializing in medical services was presented to her by the same man who told me that Sabria's branching opportunity as an ESEO was a "God thing." It was all falling into place for her, and this was what made me so emotional. I knew God was aligning my kids' lives to his ultimate plan, and it was seeing the plans revealed that had me so touched. All our kids were thriving despite us seemingly struggling. When we finally looked up, we acknowledged the fact that our older kids in the house who were sixteen and eighteen had gotten jobs and were learning how to be responsible in working, paying for their own cars and gas, which was necessary for them at their developmental levels to learn to have a good work ethic. They were balancing life and work. Sophia wanted braces, and we could not afford them at the time, so she had gotten a job and earned her own money to get braces at the age of sixteen. She made her own commitment and her own appointments for her teeth. My little ones were learning how to juggle church, school, workouts, and sports. My husband, Bobby, and I found this information out about Sabria as we were ending our prayer to God, asking him to abundantly bless us even through this storm. We asked him to guide us as we refused to see money, status, and simple jobs as our drive; but instead, we would be driven by faith and purpose. My life of faith was allowing me to dig deeper. We did raise the kids to live by faith, but now we were living it to a new level. We didn't know all that was coming or what would be changing in our lives; we just knew we were ready.

I was threatened through my time of talking out about COVID on the radio and at work. I was discriminated against and harassed for speaking truth at work, but I still did it. If I can know this about myself and all the blessings that were coming to me through the toughest times and the biggest valleys of my life, knowledge and abundant blessings can be gained by others too, and they can be empowered through the valleys instead of feeling washed out and defeated. Others too can search with the hope to find their own individual path to travel down, and in this way, we can all be inspired to survive and conquer the debilitating negative effects of corporate compliance and competing for popularity. I was asking for change in the world around me. I was asking to be part of something bigger and to be fulfilled in life. I was hoping to see this hope for kids and for those in the medical field, and God revealed the changes he was making, and they were coming from within. This way, I could be built to bring the very change I knew we all needed, including the change within myself. God is the truth, and I was being a vessel he could use to channel change.

I waited three months for the position to become available, but then I heard that they had reposted the job even though they told me the job would be mine. They didn't call me to extend the offer like they promised, another breach in trust and honesty. I realized leadership was just hoping I had moved on. Did anyone speak up for me like I did for them concerning this position? I didn't know. I hope they did, but I never got a call. What I did know was that I had outgrown that hospital, and by now there were no positions that I could find purpose in there. I knew God had me on target for my mission. I had peace about the change. I was overqualified now. I was powerful. It was time to move on to new soil to spread seed for growth and change. I knew I had planted seed there at the hospital, and that was my job. During the three months that I kept getting canceled from my shifts, I had been building my career as a jump stretch coach and was writing more books to publish as I lived by faith. I submitted a manuscript for my very first children's book, and it got approved for publication. I knew I had found my passion in writing and jump stretch, and the classes in the summer program were going great. I was connecting with the kids, and more opportunities were becoming available. After I saw what I was becoming, I said one day, on a Sunday, July 9, "I'm going to quit my job tomorrow." Bobby said, "Do it. You should have done that a while ago. They don't value you there." He hated seeing that they didn't respect me or use what was valuable in me, and now he knew he needed to buckle down and be more responsible to have my back. He had already been doing this. He saw my worth, and he was willing to work harder to support the family by having faith. He found his place too now, and he was changing. If no one else was inspired, he was. He knew who I was and who I represented. He was impressed with all I brought to the table and was willing to let me be brave and innovative to build the program God was leading me into. He began helping me with the project in any way he could. He was a team player. It wasn't them pushing me out of the hospital; it was God ushering me into my new life. So I understood all that was happening. The day I had been praying for was finally here. The next day, July 10, 2023, I quit my nursing job of nineteen years. I felt like I was reborn. I was so light I could fly. I had decided that no financial plan, retirement, pension, or spot in seniority mattered to me. It never served me well in the past, so I washed my hands of all of that and moved on. I had so much peace about it. This is the God I serve. The decision was so easy. I would have to work hard, take more steps of faith, but by now I was built for battle. I trusted God, and I knew he loved me and had a plan. I sought him at every turn. I paid attention and got to work. After the successful summer jump stretch program ended, my partner and I parted ways. She went back to her job, and I decided to move on with jump stretch opportunities as God opened doors. There was a gym owner in my town who loved my ideas of jump stretch, and he invited me to coach in his gym. I kept chipping away one day at a time, following God's lead, and before I knew it, I had all the equipment and designed the perfect stations, workouts, and lesson plans to start a program to help people learn to develop discipline, good character, self-worth, and of course, all the amazing physical benefits jump stretch offers. The details just all worked out. One day at a time, more and more things got done to make this happen. I moved in faith buying things I needed that I shouldn't have had the money to buy, but the money was there. God just kept laying out the red carpet and said, "Keep walking." He was the light on the path, teaching me and helping me to be brave and open-minded, adventurous, and willing to try new things. I had to have courage and had to trust him. I didn't need a "how to" guide. I had God. I even got the opportunity to work on furthering my education through the National Academy of Sports Medicine in personal training and nutrition and developed my very own customized compression bands for the unique ankle therapy I provided through jump stretch. They are called 33:3 bands. I was called the "real deal" in one of the towns I was coaching in, and they said I was "the talk of the town." This made me smile. This was all in just a few months after quitting that job in the hospital. I just dove right in and walked in faith into what God provided and was flooded with opportunities and blessings. I met so many wonderful people, and it was all by the grace of God. He was running the show, and He was good at it. Thank you to all the nurses who strive to love God's people, who never stop learning, making moves that benefit the world around us and who remain humble, freethinkers, brave, and loving throughout your life of service, choosing the harder right over the easier wrong. You continue to impress and motivate me. Let's continue moving in the right direction to not grow comfortable in the field but instead to continue to make big change for the better.

Life is about choices. Some people are only into building a big business. I say that is not good enough for me. You might say God built me to be in the business to build good leaders, and that means he must first build the leader within. This may take many years, and you may even be taught by people who can no longer speak at all, but to change the world around you, you must first be willing to change yourself and see the value in others even from the bedside. Be careful to listen to the stories being told around you each and every day. There are many lessons to be learned even from patients who may seem to be lost in another world and confined to a bed. They are not far from any one of us. I carry them in my spirit, and they still motivate me every day so that through my efforts, they are honored. This is how the power of God's love can transfer from nurse to patient and then back to the nurse and out to the world. To God be the glory. I am free! After all I've been through, I still have my faith, my honor, the truth, a voice, and now a new purpose.

The End

Me and my oldest daughter, Sabria, in a jump stretch class.

About the Author

Writer of *Raising West Point: The Unmasking of a Hero* and *The Tree That Could*, Christina Hunter enjoys writing inspirational stories that channel hope and teach truth. Serving as a nurse for twenty years and raising six kids, all athletes, she answered her calling to become a jump stretch coach to positively influence the world through athletics because of her hope in Jeremiah 29:11, "'For I know the plans I have for you,' declares the Lord, 'plans to prosper you and not to harm you, plans to give you hope and a future.'" She finds joy in her purpose to develop workouts and lesson plans that encourage, inspire, and train athletes to learn respect, practice autonomy, and have self-worth so they can reach their highest potential in sports and in life. Using the concepts found in the explosive and dynamic rubber band training of jump stretch and her experience as a registered nurse, Christina makes it her life's work to prevent injury, promote health, and build good character in athletes. She serves others by being an advocate, believing that if you want to make a change in the world around you, it is vital to make changes within yourself. This concept was what humbled her as a nurse, allowing her to have hope from the bedside in all circumstances while learning to respect herself and others, constantly gaining perspective. Her passion for people drove her to speak truth about the field of nursing and to write about her experiences in hopes to generate positive change both in herself and in others, attempting to resuscitate the hearts of the those who serve and are served. She loves nature, going on runs in the park with her kids, and has two pets, a cat and a dog. Her new grandson lights up her world.

Printed in the USA
CPSIA information can be obtained
at www.ICGtesting.com
CBHW032007060724
11149CB00008B/184